Nashua Public Library

Enjoy this book!

Please remember to return it on time
so that others may enjoy it too.

Manage your library account and
discover all we offer by visiting us
online at www.nashualibrary.org

Love your library? Tell a friend!

DETROIT HUSTLE

DETROIT HUSTLE

A MEMOIR OF LOVE, LIFE & HOME

AMY HAIMERL

Running Press
PHILADELPHIA · LONDON

ISBN 978-0-7624-5735-9
Library of Congress Control Number: 2015959979

E-book ISBN 978-0-7624-5744-1

10   9   8   7   6   5   4   3   2   1
Digit on the right indicates the number of this printing

Cover design by Jennifer Carrow
Interior design by Sarah Pierson
Typography: Apollo MT, Trump Gothic, Thunderhouse

Running Press Book Publishers
2300 Chestnut Street
Philadelphia, PA 19103-4371

Visit us on the web!
www.runningpress.com

To my mother . . . who loved me first
To my father . . . who loves me regardless
To my brother . . . who loves me anyway
To my husband . . . who loves me always

"There are cities that get by on their good looks, offer climate and scenery, views of mountains or oceans, rockbound or with palm trees. And there are cities like Detroit that have to work for a living."

—*Elmore Leonard*

CHAPTER ONE

I STARE THE HOUSE SQUARELY in the eye. It stares back at me, unblinking, through its boarded-up windows.

Now, I say to it, *now is the time. If you want us to build our lives here, you need to tell me now. This is your chance.*

And I don't mean I say that in my mind. No, I am standing here in the early spring bluster, speaking out loud to a 1914 Georgian Revival that hasn't seen a better day in many, many days. The neighbors must think I am crazy or, more likely, just another New Yorker scoping cheap houses in the Motor City.

I impatiently tap my foot, daring the house to answer. My husband, Karl, looks on skeptically. And then, two signs: first, a giant white tomcat walks across the roof and stares at us, and second, as dusk settles over the city, a streetlight comes on. In a town known for its lack of working streetlights—and nearly every other city service—a puddle of gold is forming right outside what could be our window.

Karl and I look at each other expectantly, silently hoping the other one is going to do or say the sensible thing. Like walk away.

The house is a three-thousand-square-foot box of fuckeduped-ness. It has no plumbing. No electricity. No heat. And I don't mean it's just missing a toilet or a boiler—there is essentially nothing left inside the walls. Every pipe, every radiator, every wire is stripped. Every door is missing. Every light fixture is long gone. There is no water heater, no furnace. There are no kitchen cabinets or sink. No stove, no refrigerator. What we have is a pile of bricks with character. Let's be honest: the house could be used as a set for *Falling Skies* or any other postapocalyptic show.

Still, we are inexplicably smitten. We can already imagine our lives inside these walls, despite the peeling Pepto-Bismol pink paint, sagging ceilings, mold-speckled surfaces, and sunroom that is shedding its stucco and letting the wind and rain inside. Karl mentally places his Baldwin grand piano in that room and imagines it bathed in late-summer twilight. I hear him playing the jazz standards and rolling blues he's partial to as I cook dinner using tomatoes and basil grown from an imaginary garden right outside his floor-to-ceiling windows. For now, though, it is just that: imagination. Every window is boarded over, the entire place shrouded in musty darkness punctuated only by the occasional crack of light, dust motes dancing in the stream. We use the glow of our iPhones to inspect the damage, a little trepidatious to walk through the house. We don't even want to step into Karl's future music room because we fear the water-logged floorboards might collapse under our weight.

We venture up the staircase, which has the appearance of bad dental work thanks to all the missing and cracked balusters. We're cautious on the first few steps, testing them gingerly to see whether they hold. They do. Rocks and glass litter the cracked linoleum steps. As we walk past the stairwell window, we see tiny holes in the glass, evidence of how the debris came to be.

On the second floor the windows are mostly intact and unboarded, so we can actually see what lies before us. To our left are two bedrooms, one of which seems to be in decent condition. Although that's a lot like saying Velveeta is better than government cheese; there's only the finest line of difference. The better room has a hole in the center of the floor and features layers of peeling plaster and wallpaper. My favorite is a tiny 1940s-era floral print that peeps through in places.

This, I think, *has potential*. We could live in this room while we're renovating. I know the rule: take one room and make it your own. Frances Mayes taught me that lesson years ago when I read her book *Under the Tuscan Sun*. And again when I watched the movie, cheering on Diane Lane as she lovingly scoured a medallion of the Virgin Mary on her bed frame. I suddenly see myself in that movie, this house as my own Tuscan villa. *How hard can it be?* I think. *Frances did it*. (In my head we are on a first-name basis. I met her at a book signing once, so it's not totally crazy-town.)

Across the hall is the master bedroom and bathroom. Well, at least we think it is. This space is baffling: it is a warren of rooms that appear to have once housed a bedroom, a bathroom, and maybe a kitchen. There is a hole busted through the wall separating the bathroom and the "kitchen"—all the better to pass martinis and snacks to the person in the bath, perhaps? Where a tub once stood is now just a gaping maw. The sunporch is even more mold infested and rickety looking than Karl's piano room directly below.

"Maybe someone had tenants up here at one point?" Karl suggests. "It would explain that weird staircase coming up the back side of the house."

Regardless, it all has to go.

We walk upstairs to the attic, which is a completely raw space, bare down to the studs. The floorboards are rough and you can see where they were once encased in linoleum. But on each side of the house is a dormer with windows opening up onto the Detroit skyline. To the south I can see the Detroit River through the trees. I wonder whether, in the winter, I'll be able to watch the barges and freighters slip by. I just know if I strain my ears, I'll be able to hear the sounds of buoy bells and the forlorn call of a foghorn. I imagine a library up here in the eaves, an overstuffed chair tucked into one of the dormers so I can while away the afternoon, novels tugging me into imaginary worlds. *This*, I think, *is my favorite room.*

Karl and I make our way back downstairs, slowly descending into the darkness in search of the kitchen. We finally identify it only because there is nowhere else a kitchen could be. The space is actually a nest of rooms all connected to one another through random doorways, each so tight and cramped it feels like a prairie dog town. The walls are painted the color of lemon meringue pie, and neither of us can figure out where a refrigerator might have gone or how anyone actually cooked in here. There is a tiny vestibule that you could call a mudroom except that "room" is too generous a description; I'm not sure you could have two humans in it at once. I see many dog-human-coffee-leash fiascos happening here. Right now it is home to one rolling office chair and two Pepsi bottles filled with urine, signs of a former—or possibly current—squatter.

I try the back door and discover that it is nailed shut from the outside. It wouldn't have mattered: the house lacks a set of stairs to the ground. For now it is a door to nowhere.

Karl comes up from the basement to inform me that he found a toilet but is certain I don't want to see it. There is also a small brick room that would be a perfect cellar, its cool, dry environment useful for storing cases of wine as well as the pints of tomatoes, peaches, pickles, and jams I am already dreaming of canning each summer.

We walk outside to discover a long, lush backyard dotted with original gas lamps. Small purple globes of clover peek up through the grass. Maple trees and box elders line the yard on one side, shading a picturesque, ivy-covered carriage house. The remnants of a once-tended flower garden are evident, with spring bulbs sprouting and the heads of early daffodils bobbing in the wind. At the back of the long lot stands a three-car garage, its roof punctured by tree branches, that appears to be sinking into itself. Still, we look at each other in awe. We are not yet contemplating the maintenance and upkeep this yard will require; we are imagining the sparkling parties we could host.

The house is certainly nothing like what we imagined back home in Brooklyn. It's only been eight months since we left, but it feels like a lifetime ago. Back then Karl and I would often dream of a more sustainable life where we could try to open a business or work on a creative project without going bankrupt. We loved our neighborhood of Red Hook and couldn't imagine leaving, but we also couldn't imagine staying. Our rent was topping $3,500 a month, and we were working just to keep our middle-class life afloat. We'd be deep into the evening, after a third nightcap or so, and we'd pull up Google Maps and talk about where we'd go. I wanted New Orleans, but the South is too hot for my Tennessee-born spouse. We talked about the West, but I wasn't ready to return home to Denver. Most of California was out. Cleveland? Detroit without the cache. Philly? Maybe. Portland or Seattle? Hell, no. No tourist towns, with their happy lattes and endless bike lanes. Yes, those things are lovely and we enjoy them, but we wanted a place that was forging its future, not relaxing on its accomplishments. We wanted a working-class town with an entre-preneurial spirit.

Inevitably we would land on Detroit and the powerful lure of its cheap real estate. We fantasized about buying something small and quaint, fixing it up, and then enjoying a comfortable life with two salaries and no mortgage. We fancied ourselves economic refugees crashing on the shores of the Detroit River, coming to buy our free-dom and future. But it was always just an idea, a possibility tucked safe within our minds. We were talking about Detroit in the dreamy way that New Yorkers always discuss other, less expensive locales and how much better it must be there. It's an idea, a game. You never actually do it.

Until you do. And then you find yourself standing in a city you barely know, in a neighborhood you can't pinpoint on a map, talking to a house that's most recent tenant was a raccoon.

We must be crazy. We have no family here, no ties to Detroit. Who moves to the murder capital of America to make a home and build a life?

A man walks across the street toward us, waving.

"Hi," he says. "I'm Jim Boyle."

Jim has lived across the street from this house for the past fifteen years, and it has been his nemesis for many of those years. He and the other neighbors have had to deal with boarding it up, mowing the grass, and doing their best to arrest the decay. They are desperate for someone to bring this house back to life and end the cycle of vandalism and squatting taking place on one of the best blocks in the city.

The house stands as an aging sentry on this quiet, leafy block on Detroit's east side. It is the last empty house to be found on Van Dyke Place in the historic West Village neighborhood, so named because it sits just to the west of the ritzier, more glamorous Indian Village. That neighborhood is known for its extravagant mansions with carriage houses and ballrooms that were once home to the likes of Edsel Ford and Henry Leland, the founders of Lincoln and Cadillac. Meanwhile, the West Village is the more middle-class sibling—though one with its own listing on the National Register of Historic Places. Both factory workers and the former secretary of the Navy have called these blocks home, dwelling in gracious Queen Annes, Victorian townhomes, and modest duplexes all tucked beneath a canopy of trees. Even the apartment buildings boast three-story Ionic porticos and intricate stone carving on the façades, hinting to an era when the city was flush with cash and had a penchant for the ornate.

Still, even here there are signs of the struggles that have beset Detroit. The sidewalks are buckled and cracked. Abandoned homes sit open and exposed, their tender underbellies ravaged by the weather and human desperation. Even occupied homes seem to be starving for attention and maintenance. Gutters sigh heavy in the wind, and melted vinyl siding provides lasting evidence of the frequent fires. The nearest retail establishment is a party store (Michigan-speak for a bodega or off-brand 7-Eleven) or the gas station two blocks away that serves up bait and tackle along with diesel and unleaded. Vacant, weed-infested lots spread like a virus around the edges of the West

Village, and the main approach to the area is cloaked in darkness because there isn't a single working streetlight for blocks.

But we can also see the love just below the surface. Lawns are cut. Porches swept. Gardens planted. The empty lot next door to the house is maintained as the neighbors fight Detroit's tall prairie grasses, which can absorb a place as quickly as the kudzu of the South.

"What are your plans?" Jim Boyle asks. "Are you going to live in the house?"

His tone makes it clear that there is only one correct answer.

"Yes?" we reply, looking at each other and wondering what we have just committed to.

"You'll be fine. You can do this," Jim says. "My wife and I did ours, like, fifteen years ago. It'll be great."

CHAPTER TWO

DETROIT SMELLS LIKE HOME.

The warm sweetness of prairie grasses baking in the summer sun transports me back to the fields behind my grandparents' house. The almost licentious smell of the earth after an evening rainstorm is that of freshly irrigated crops. The intoxicating scent of honeysuckle vines climbing up chain-link fences and corrugated metal walls recalls the construction sites and scrap yards of my childhood. Rich wood smoke, curling through Detroit's sharp winter skies, is the smell of safety, of my mother. Grease, dirt, and sweat mix together to create the same musky scent of work that was always caught in my dad's Carhartts. The smells of my past mingle with my future, overlapping and intertwining like a jazz riff so that Detroit seems inevitable now, as if I'd been searching for this place since before I knew I was looking.

My hometown of Fruita, Colorado, is a place that feels like it's a thousand miles from nowhere. It sits almost at the Utah border, nestled in the Grand Valley, boxed in by gray shale cliffs to the north and red rock canyons to the south. The snow-capped Rocky Mountains rise in the distant eastern sky as the great Utah desert encroaches from the west. My mother describes it as the "lunar landscape"—when she's being generous—but there is great beauty in its harshness. Fruita, like Detroit, is not an easy or obvious place to love. They do not inspire poetry and serenades on first meeting. They are places that unfold slowly and whisper their secrets. It is the way the moonlight catches a rock face of the Bookcliffs or the majesty of a pheasant taking flight at dawn, with Detroit's art deco skyline in the distance. There is hardship writ everywhere in both of my spiritual homes, and they are connected, for me, across space and time by scent and the sound of the meadowlark's song on the wind.

How my truck-driver father convinced my middle-class mother to move from Denver and into his single-wide trailer in Fruita is as much a mystery now as me being drawn to Detroit. It seems implausible on the surface, but they were living on love. I was just four when we moved in with him, and the trailer was so tiny that I slept on the living room couch, lulled to sleep by the sound of train whistles calling across the night and their headlights dancing across the walls.

The mythology of the area is that the Ute Indians cursed the valley after being forced off their land and onto Utah reservations. It certainly felt cursed at times. In the summer the heat shimmered off the pavement by 10 a.m., so my mother and I always left early to run errands. If we didn't beat the heat, we'd be peeling our legs off the bench seat of Dad's 1973 Ford Highboy. The winter was equally brutal. I rode my bike to school each day, wearing a Union Bay fleece, head tucked into the funnel neck to protect my face from the biting wind. Riding blind, I ran my red Schwinn ten-speed into the back of so many parked cars that I bent the fork. After the fifty-eleventh time fixing that bike, my father threatened to take it away if I couldn't be more careful. The next time I crashed, careening into a ditch, I learned to ride with a wobble rather than admit what had happened. I couldn't lose that bike; it was my prized possession. I'd spent all summer hunting cans roadside, crushing them, and recycling the metal to afford an upgrade from the Huffy boy's bike that my dad scavenged from the desert behind my grandparents' place.

My life plan was to marry the neighbor boy and live in his chicken coop. I don't remember what kind of wedding I thought we would have—I was never that kind of girl, the one who dreams of dresses, flowers, and first-dance songs—but I thought Travis was kind, thoughtful, and funny. Or maybe I just liked his chickens. Either way, marriage was all that was expected of girls like me, living on the far western edge of Colorado in single-wide trailers, not even well-to-do enough to boast of double-wides. Husband. Babies. Cashier at the City Market. That would have been my future if Dick Haimerl had been a different kind of man.

But he told me I could be anything, do anything. I learned to read sitting next to him in the red Kenworth truck, hauling heavy loads across the West. His boss, Old Man Hall, didn't allow kids in his rigs, but Dad would occasionally sneak me along. I would crouch on the floorboards, and he would toss a blanket over my head until we passed the gates. Then it was him and I and the open road. Willie Nelson, C. W. McCall, and Crystal Gayle were the soundtrack to my childhood. I would sit next to him for hours, piecing together words out of local newspapers picked up in truck stops along the way. My dad's constant encouragement—despite what he told me later could be tedious and painful hours—became the foundation of our relationship and his way of helping a daughter grow beyond what he could imagine. After all, nobody in his family had gone to college, and women in particular weren't encouraged in that direction.

From the very beginning I was a daddy's girl. That Dick wasn't legally mine didn't matter to either of us. My mother has always said that if I were given the choice, I would love her but choose him. I was happier out of doors with Dad, sorting nuts and bolts or fetching tools, than inside with my mother. One summer he and I built a flat-bed trailer together, from the axles up.

"Hey, squirt," he'd say at the end of each day, inspecting our work-in-progress. "Go grab us a couple of Pepsis from your mom."

We would sit there together in the shade of the elm, legs dangling from atop the steel frame we'd erected.

Those were the good years, a brief period of bounty before the tough times hit. And when they hit, they hit hard and fast. One day Exxon was planning a huge investment in the area, touting the Grand Valley's shale cliffs as America's way of becoming energy independent. The next day Exxon was gone. It pulled out overnight, having decided the oil was too expensive to extract. The company took a hit on its quarterly earnings, a tiny blip in its stock price, but in the valley May 2, 1982 was Black Sunday. More than two thousand people had no job to report to on Monday morning. By the end of the summer more than 10 percent of the county's population had fled.

It was a recession that old-timers said rivaled the Great Depression. Exxon's decision rippled out across the economy, causing suppliers, retail businesses, restaurants—everything—to close their doors and board their windows. Maco, the company my father worked for, went out of business too, and he got the first pink slip of many to come. But Maco gave my family a parting gift: close down the shop, they told my father, and we'll sell you the scraps, whatever you want, cheap. Hell, they said, you can take most of it for free. He sorted through the remains of the business, collecting things that, to anyone else's eye, looked like junk: pipe, scrap metal, fittings, bolts, screws, even an office chair. He brought it all home to the tiny house my parents had purchased just before the bust and squirreled it all away for some unseen future. He didn't know what use he would have for the parts and pieces, but he knew you never turn down opportunity.

"You have to hustle, kid," he said. "Always hustle harder than anyone else."

His advice seems fitting now, living in a city where the unofficial motto is "Detroit hustles harder" and everybody has a main hustle, a side hustle, a creative hustle—whatever it takes to get by.

As everyone else around us fled the valley, we stayed. For five job-less years Dad made the weekly drive into Grand Junction, the nearest city, where he would fill out the unemployment forms, humiliated and dejected when he returned home. Seeing this proud man, one of the last stoic sons of the West, brought low was painful to watch, even as a kid.

Occasionally he would luck into work, but we always knew it was temporary. On those mornings I'd wave to him as he pulled the Ford out onto the county road and wonder where he was headed. Sometimes it was deep into the Rocky Mountains to fight coal fires. When that happened, he'd be away for weeks at a time while Mom and I got used to him being more of a ghost than a real person. Other times he was lucky enough to find work at the nearby refinery. The stench of that place—rotten eggs, ammonia, and burnt matches—came home in his clothes and in his borrowed work truck, which we nicknamed the Stinkmobile. No matter how many times Mom and I washed and Windexed it, we could never get the smell out. Today, when I drive past the refinery in Detroit, sometimes I can pick up the smell, and it makes me think of him.

We heated the house with wood we cut during the summers. My mother would wake in the early light to start the fire and get our house warm enough for me to dress for school. In spring and summer she grew a garden, filling the earth with corn, tomatoes, carrots, peas, beans, pumpkins. She fretted over her few extravagances: a lilac bush and finicky fuchsias. Each morning I sat on my swing set, the one Dad welded together out of scrap pipe from Maco, watching her work the rows as the dew burned off the grass. Our three-legged cocker spaniel, Bear, followed behind her, his long ears dragging in the dirt, patient and obedient until he hit the onion patch. He never could resist digging up the onions. By fall the metal pantry shelves were packed with quarts of glistening orbs—peaches, tomatoes, apricots—and jewel-like pints of jams and pickles. She learned all of the homesteading skills that had served families on this land for generations, skills she had never expected to learn but came to love and hoped to pass on to me.

Mom began buying two-pound boxes of Saltine crackers because, for one, they made a cheap dessert slathered with butter and jam. But more importantly, they were her talisman against the bad times. The first time she bought the big box—an accident—Dad didn't come home on Friday with a pink slip. When you're on the edge, you find signs anywhere you can.

I learned not to ask for anything because I didn't want to see the heartbreak in my mother's eyes. Arby's, to this day, is one of my guilty pleasures because Mom took me there for lunch on the rare occasions we had extra money for Super Roast Beefs—with Arby's Sauce, of course—and potato cakes. That was the year Mom gave me a library card for Christmas, a gift I used so frequently the town librarian soon had to order books from Denver for me to devour. Dad and I gave Mom a tiny wishing well he whittled out of a tree branch: wishing for better times.

In the depths of this poverty Dick Haimerl chose to make me legally his. He forgave my biological father's back child support—$7,000 and change—in exchange for the right to adopt me. Dad likes to say he bought me. He also likes to think he is funny.

"You were a damned good bargain, kid," he says.

Because that's him: hide the depth of your emotions under humor, deflect. Make something big seem smaller and less important, even when it is one of the most monumental things that will happen in either of your lives.

I was ten when it happened, and I remember snippets, pictures in my head, of that morning before the judge. Mom taming my flyaways and cleaning my face with her spit-damped hand—being Mama Kitty, she called it—as she reminds me not to be nervous and to just answer the man's questions. The dark wood chambers with a hush more choking than church. The man calling my name and asking me whether I want Dick Haimerl to be my dad.

I do.

When Dad stands up, the hat that was resting on his knee falls to the floor.

Afterward we went out to a dinner I knew was special because everything came on plates instead of in wrappers. There was a salad bar, the old-fashioned kind with a sneeze guard, brightly lit in the center of the room. Dad took my hand and we walked up to it. The mounted heads of dead animals watched us through glass eyes. He handed me a heavy plate and started teaching me how to build a proper tower of salad. Start with your base, the lettuce, then add the layers: cucumbers, tomatoes, cheese, beets, eggs.

"Squirt," he said, spooning something over his salad I'd never seen. "Never skimp on the bacon bits."

For several years Dad and I would celebrate my adoption day. We would sit in the shade of the great cottonwood trees, Dairy King burgers and fries between us. But at a certain point, I can't really say when, we started skipping the day, forgetting it altogether. After all, what is the point of celebrating the fact that someone is your dad, other than to remind you both that it wasn't always that way?

Times did eventually get better for Fruita, though not until long after we'd left for Golden, a small town near Denver. My hometown is now filled with tourists and mountain bikers riding all over the buttes, bluffs, and cliffs that we four-wheeled into and picnicked on, cactus blazing bright against the red earth. Lattes and gourmet pizza abound in what were once boarded-up storefronts. But it was the hardscrabble version of the town that defined me. Rural Colorado seeped into my very being; the people's resilience and determination, their sheer force of will to make something out of nothing, infected me.

The irony is that even though I'm a fifth-generation Colorado native, my lineage comes through my mother's suburban-dwelling, middle-class parents. My Wild West, rodeo-riding, truck-driving, country-music-listening, whiskey-shooting redneck dad's family are newcomers by comparison. Yet theirs is my identity, a blue-collar chip on my shoulder that speaks of coming from a hard place that few could imagine, let alone understand.

Except maybe a Detroiter. The specifics are different, of course, but Detroit, too, is a place filled with fighters who know what it means to be one of the last people standing when everyone around you has forgotten you, left you for dead, whether that's the auto industry or Exxon. They know what it means to get back up and keep swinging. Every. Damn. Time. They know what it is to believe that better days are ahead, even when all you have to build that future out of are the scraps of economic collapse. My rural Colorado father raised himself a Detroit daughter without ever imagining that the places could be culturally connected.

Of course, I haven't always embraced these blue-collar roots, worn them with defiance and pride. When we left Fruita, I wanted to rid myself of any vestiges that spoke of want and longing, to never tell of the homemade clothes and the whittled Christmas presents. When I moved to New York City in the late 1990s, I desperately wanted to reinvent myself, as so many people go to New York to do. It was the era of newly flush tech entrepreneurs, AOL buying Time Warner, and decadent parties with the ubiquitous sushi girls—naked women laid out on tables and covered in raw fish. Everyone wanted to get in on the new economy, and I was determined to fake it until I made it. Whatever "it" was.

Still, I felt so lost for the first few months that I cried myself to sleep most nights, wondering whether I'd made a terrible mistake. I cried walking down the sidewalk, feeling both overwhelmed and exhilarated. I even cried standing in the aisles of a Gristedes because I couldn't find the brown sugar. I scoured the aisles for what seemed like an eternity before discovering that this staple is sold in boxes, not bags, in New York City. Even the basics, what should have been familiar and easy, were foreign and exotic here. I eventually found my way, as everyone does. After all, it had taken some hustle and chutzpa to get there, and hustle and chutzpa work well in the Big Apple. I am the only person in my family to go to college, and I wasn't exactly knocking on Manhattan's door with an Ivy League calling card. I went to a school that accepts anyone with a pulse. (That's not hyperbole.) But I was thrilled to go at all because I didn't have the cash to pay for the fancy schools that accepted me. Nobody told my parents that the list price in college brochures isn't what you pay if you're a family in need.

It was in college that I met Donna Ladd, my first mentor and the woman who would change so many things for me. An audacious, six-foot-tall blonde from Mississippi, she was born to an alcoholic father and an illiterate mother who wanted so much better for her. We bonded instantly, even though I wasn't old enough to legally drink and she was already in her thirties. She showed me the early ropes to tapping into your past and letting it propel you to your future. She was the guide up the class ladder that my parents didn't know how to climb. And I was enthralled with her stories. She escaped her circumstances as soon as she could, going to college at Mississippi State University and eventually landing in New York City's East Village during the 1980s, where she started her own newspaper. I hung on her every word about the squatters and the riots and the cops and how she was there in the fray, telling their stories. I dreamed I could do that someday, too.

She helped me get my first job post-college as the editor-in-chief of the *Colorado Springs Business Journal*, and when she went to New

York City to work on her master's degree at Columbia University, I followed along. I scored a job as the managing editor of *Silicon Alley Reporter*, covering that crazy tech-money-fueled world. In two short years I became the executive editor of *Gotham* and *Hamptons* magazines. Sure, they were party-picture books, derided by journalists everywhere, but I was just brash enough to believe I could bring real journalism to their pages. I felt like I had arrived. I was mostly in the office, but I lived the life of gowns and parties—the same ones Mom and I once read about in *W* and *Vogue*—vicariously through our pages. I edited columns by Donald Trump and Spike Lee and assigned stories about the blueblood ladies of the Hamptons. I wrangled celebrity interviews, and Paris Hilton was technically our intern (though I only actually saw her once).

Still, the irony was lost on nobody, least of all me, that a girl from a trailer in Colorado was telling the wealthy how to spend their riches. So for my first big party I knew I had to represent. I found a Prada dress at a consignment shop and spent almost a month's rent on it. I felt fabulous as I walked into the party.

A woman approached me, champagne in hand.

"Great dress," she said. "Too bad it's so three seasons ago."

It felt like I'd been sucker punched. I'd been outed as a fraud. Everyone there knew I was just a girl who was supposed to marry the boy in the trailer.

◆ ◆ ◆

When the terrorist attacks of 9/11 tore a gash in the city's psyche and reality a few short weeks later, it changed everything in an instant. The publishing industry, which was already in a state of flux as the Internet began its rise, started hemorrhaging jobs, mine included, and the fast money of the dot-com boom dried up. I tried to hold out, scrape by on unemployment benefits, but when your studio rent is more than your unemployment and you have no trust fund and no fall-back plan, there aren't a lot of options. I felt like a failure.

Sensing my struggle, Donna suggested I come visit her in Jackson, Mississippi, and get a change of scenery from the oppressive gray of February in New York. She and her partner, Todd, had moved down there the previous year after she completed her master's thesis about her hometown of Philadelphia, Mississippi, where Edgar Ray Killen and the Ku Klux Klan executed three civil rights workers—James Earl Chaney, Michael Schwerner, and Andrew Goodman—on a summer night in 1964. They were registering African Americans to vote, and Donna was just a child. She never expected to go home, back South to those stories, but she suddenly felt compelled to stay and possibly start a newspaper. She thought maybe I could help.

I hopped on the mighty Amtrak Crescent, with daily trips "from the Big Apple to the Big Easy." *South toward home?* I wondered, the inverse of Willie Morris's "North Toward Home." We chugged out of Penn Station, through the rolling hills of Virginia, past Hotlanta, and finally into Meridian, Mississippi, the doldrums shaking loose with each latitude deeper south.

The air was soft and warm as I stepped off the train and saw Donna waving from the black topless Miata, her long hair seeming to cast light. The magnolia trees were about to burst open, and the entire place smelled verdant. I soaked in that lushness, drinking in the unknown, the mysterious. As the car zipped along the road, the yellow dotted line spooling out before us, it felt as if Mississippi was unfurling its beauty and secrets just for me.

Donna knew the sway of the South, knew the power of its whisper. All she had to do was let it entice me. She introduced me around town and took me to watch Myrlie Evers donate her late husband Medgar's papers to the state of Mississippi. She gave away his writings, his essence, in the very chambers where that state voted to secede from the union over slavery. It was such a powerful and moving moment, filled with grace, that I sobbed as I watched, even though I didn't know the story. I didn't know who this civil rights leader was. I didn't know the tragic story of Byron De La Beckwith Jr. creeping up on Evers's house in the darkness of a June morning in 1963, hate filling his heart, and shooting Evers in his driveway. When Donna took me to tour the house where it had happened, I pressed my thumb into a divot in the refrigerator, evidence of where one bullet had ricocheted. She told me about the South's history of White Citizen Councils and Jim Crow laws and everything else I had not learned in school.

I knew much of class and poverty, but growing up in rural Colorado and coming of age in metro Denver, my world had been very white and Hispanic. I knew of Native Americans and our country's abhorrent treatment of them. I knew of living in borderlands and in-between places. I knew of outsiders and struggle. But the history of African Americans and even the civil rights movement was something else. Walking through the door of Medgar Evers's house opened a world to me, and Donna made sure that I looked in, that I committed to understanding, to learning, to reading. We had been drawn together, despite a nearly fifteen-year age difference, mentor and mentee, as people who wanted to make a difference, change the world, face injustice and inequality in the world. To write about it and expose it and give new voices the chance to speak.

I went back to New York, sublet my apartment, and moved to Mississippi. The plan was for me to stay and help write a business plan for the publication and work on a sample issue in exchange for free rent. That would buy me time to explore my next steps and decide whether Mississippi was the home I wanted it to be. I was a 100 percent convert to the struggles and beauties of the place. And not because I didn't recognize the challenges but because I did, and I was inspired by the people and their herculean efforts to structure their world.

Helping write the business plan for *Jackson Free Press* is one of my proudest accomplishments. Donna and Todd have stayed in Jackson, building that paper into a media powerhouse for Mississippi. Its journalism is award winning, and it is known for investigative work that put an old Klansman in prison and a corrupt mayor on trial. Their story is the one I tell young journalists now, showing them what our profession is supposed to be, as opposed to just BuzzFeed and Gawker. I tell them to read *The Reconstruction of a Racist*, a biography of Hodding Carter Jr., to understand the power we as media have to influence and change hearts and minds. We can be the force of good, not just cat videos. (Though I love those too!)

But financial realities like student loans meant I couldn't stay forever. Eventually my unemployment benefits would run out, and Donna couldn't yet afford to pay me. So when a job at *Westword*, the alt-weekly in Denver, opened up, I applied. I'd always dreamed of working with the legendary Patty Calhoun, who had started the newspaper more than three decades earlier and was still helming it and rabble-rousing every single day. And Denver was the first city I fell in love with. I still remember the day the affair began: my grandmother had taken me downtown to visit my aunt Cindy for lunch, and the tall towers and building canyons captured my imagination. I wanted to grow up and live there; I couldn't imagine anything more glamorous. As a teenager, I plied the dark sides of those same streets, frequenting the Goth bars and punk clubs, drinking coffee at 2 a.m. at Muddy's or Paris on the Platte when I was supposed to be any-where but in those all-night joints. In college it became my city, the one where I worked and played and loved. And now it was pulling me back, a place of unfinished business.

◆ ◆ ◆

Everyone has that relationship. That man or woman who leaves us scared and devastated and possibly even financially ruined. The one we couldn't say no to, couldn't resist, just kept chasing like he or she was one more hit of the good stuff, as Veronica Mars would say.

My mistake was called Sean.

We'd met when I was a sophomore in college. He was seven years my senior, but that didn't matter; I'd always dated older men. I didn't find him handsome exactly, but something drew me to him. Com-pelled me to him. When he shared a collection of romantic short stories he had written, I swooned. He was so romantic and soulful.

I was so young.

So when Sean called late one night, telling a sob story of how he'd lost the keys to the place he was crashing at, of course I offered to let him stay with me.

He showed up an hour later and never left.

At first it was fun, like playing house. We were in our own insu-lar world where all we needed was each other. We'd lay in bed for hours talking about everything, debating politics, and dreaming of the future together. But it didn't last.

I will spare you all of the gory details of how bad it got other than to say it became a death spiral of lying and cheating, on both our sides, that left me financially ruined. I should have listened to my cat, Ben, who peed on Sean's jeans that very first night.

But I didn't. I would like to say Sean trapped me back in our dysfunctional relationship, but the truth is that I propelled myself. Moving to New York had been the only way I could break free from the cycle. And here I was, not only going back to Denver but thinking about going back to him.

Sean thought we could do it right this time. He'd gotten his life together while I was away. He had his own apartment and had built a remodeling company. I was wary, but I saw the changes in him. And I, too, had changed. I was more confident and firm in what I wanted. Even Donna, who never liked Sean, saw the changes and thought maybe it could work. I told myself that our troubled years were going to be a funny anecdote in our origin story, a blip in an epic love story.

I should have gotten my own place, taken it slow. But I've never been one for half-measures or appropriate caution.

Instead, I got the house bug.

I was in my midtwenties, in a committed relationship, and had a professional career—well, as professional as you can call a job at a paper that both won national awards for its reporting and featured sex ads in the back. If you know you don't want to have kids and you're neutral at best about marriage, what's the next logical step? Real estate, of course.

Sean and I had no money, no savings, and no real way to pay for a house. But it was 2003, and the housing bubble was forming. I didn't know that the price escalation and underlying bad mortgages would eventually collapse the US economy and devastate cities from Detroit to San Francisco; all I knew is that I was fifth-generation native to Denver and that prices were quickly soaring out of my range. Hell, they were already way beyond it. And I wanted a small piece of my city to call home.

We tried to be responsible. We sought a house we could afford on just my salary so that if Sean's work as a contractor was unsteady, we wouldn't have to worry. That capped our budget at roughly $100,000 and seriously limited our options. Even my beloved Capitol Hill, where I'd lived while in college, was completely out of our range. When I'd first moved there for college in 1993, my mother was so afraid of the neighborhood that I invented fake boundaries and convinced her that the drugs and prostitution were "over there," far from my $250-a-month apartment. That was when I could have bought the castle-looking house next door to my apartment for what seems like Detroit prices today. In 1992, the year before I moved in, the house sold for $65,000. A year later it was back on the market for $225,000. A decade later, as Sean and I started our search, that same house sold for nearly half a million dollars.

If the cheap college area, where students and artists had always flocked, wasn't in our budget, where was? We looked north to the skid-row neighborhoods, which were becoming a pressure valve for people like us looking to capture some small part of Denver for themselves. The environment didn't have much to recommend it, from a middle-class yuppie perspective, which is what most of the neighbors initially perceived us to be. There was no Whole Foods or grocery store, just a corner store selling loosies and Virgin Mary candles. But the Victorians and tiny bungalows appealed to us.

When we finally found our home, it was one of those Sean's kit-type houses that were built across the West at the turn of the twentieth century. You could order your home from a catalog, and they would load up the material and ship it via boxcar. All you had to do was assemble onsite. Somebody decided to do that in 1900, erecting an 826-square-foot brick home on the edge of downtown Denver, at the headwater of Larimer Street, where Jack Kerouac had haunted during the summer of 1947. Kerouac stayed only briefly in Denver, just ten days, a side note in a journal, but he and Neal Cassady crawled up and down Welton and Larimer and Curtis Streets, jazzing in the Five Points district, the poetry of the streets running through his mind wouldn't stop, couldn't stop. He told America about it in *On the Road*, forever intertwining his destiny with the Queen City of the Plains.

But my house, those neighborhoods, were not among the city's jewels. Ours was the second-cheapest property on the Denver market at the time, a mere $115,000. The cheapest one, clocking in at $98,000, was just up the block and so cockroach infested that after touring it, I felt phantom bugs crawling on my skin for days. The Cole neighborhood was "in transition," as realtors like to say, with a light rail line stop in the imminent future and a great burger joint around the way, though realtors didn't make Jeffrey Patterson and his delicious, pancake-sized Caro's Corner burgers part of their spiel. The dilapidated former auto body shop that housed Caro's was perhaps a bit too real.

It would take twenty minutes or more for Jeffrey to fry you up a meal, but he would stand there behind the grill and bullshit with you, talking sports, usually. He played college football, or maybe he boxed, I don't rightly remember, not sure I latched on to the fact then, as sports clueless as I am. But Sean, who played a touch of college ball, could chat with him for hours. I remember his booming laughter that filled the room in which the only seating was a church pew with a few Bibles stacked up for good measure.

One Caro burger would kill your arteries, but it would only set you back $4.04. It was a steal. Sean and I became regulars, the odd white folk coming in and out of a place that most didn't venture far enough outside downtown to find. Jeffrey embraced us immediately, and I set to designing and printing his take-out menus and helping with other clerical needs. In exchange he gave us legitimacy with our new neighbors, a stamp of approval indicating we were willing to live, eat, and walk in the neighborhood, not just hide out in the loft development up the street with its gated parking lot like so many of the other new faces.

Sean and I showed up at closing for our house ready to sign our life away, committing to a thirty-year adjustable rate mortgage with a 7 percent interest rate that could flex up after two years. We didn't pay too much attention to that last fact. The payment was less than we were shelling out in rent, so we thought we were golden. We knew the specter of rising interest rates was out there, but we planned to renovate the house, mostly cosmetic stuff like pulling up the carpet and repainting, and then refinance into a solid thirty-year, fixed-rate loan. The American gold standard.

The next thing I knew I was crushing a sledgehammer through the wall, not so much repainting as taking the house down to its studs and rebuilding. Sean decided we could rework the antiquated floor plan—one where you had to walk through the master bedroom to get to the only bathroom—and make the house worth more in case we ever decided to sell. And if we were going to do that, we might as well rewire and replumb while the walls were open. There was talk of excavating the dirt out of the unfinished basement to fulfill his dreams of a man cave and wine cellar.

In the interim, though, I dreamed of a functioning kitchen and running water. It is a dream familiar to almost anyone who has bought a house in Detroit. When we first moved in, we had to flush the toilet with a bucket and drive to the truck stop to take showers. When we did finally get water, it was in a bath. Our daily hygiene ritual involved filling a tub with water, running out of hot water before the tub was full, and taking a tepid soak. To this day I'm no fan of baths. Showers, that's the thing.

Eventually Sean and I would replace the plumbing, the sewer line, and the hot water heater after the original broke down for good on, of course, a cold winter morning. My best friend, Stacy Cowley, who I met at *Silicon Alley Reporter* and who has stuck by me through every folly, wouldn't want me to forget to mention the whole-house water-filtration system that Sean insisted we buy from a door-to-door salesman for $6,000. She is still bitter about that on my behalf, while I've chalked it up to a life lesson and my inability to say no to Sean.

We sanded the hardwood floors and stained them a gorgeous rich red, custom mixed by Sean, and then brushed on at least five layers of polycoating to bring out their depth. They were a work of art. Sean spent nights sanding the walls with only a black light in order to achieve museum-quality flat falls. Any texture reminds me of the popcorn walls of my childhood, the cheap sprayed-on kind that were in all my friends' homes, stained yellow with nicotine and coated in dust and cooking grease. No, we would have flat walls. He would have charged a client $100 an hour for the work.

We encased the closets in cedar, and Sean milled custom, historically accurate trim for around the windows, doors, and baseboards. We took down the chain-link fence and replaced it with cedar tongue-and-groove panels and posts topped with copper hats. We landscaped the entire yard, putting in new grass and pavers, growing hollyhock, black-eyed Susans, purple coneflower, and succulents, all the drought-tolerant plants that spring up with gorgeous color in the high plains desert of Denver.

And while we were working away, time got away from us. The two-year fixed-rate period on the mortgage went by quickly, and suddenly we were facing a rising bill. Our interest rate would eventually top out at nearly 13 percent and eat up almost my entire monthly paycheck.

Yet we kept pouring money into the house. We didn't think about or plan for the costs so much as just scrounge money where we could. Because we were doing the work ourselves, no one expense seemed that large, no one thing seemed like the place to draw the line. Like most people rehabbing houses this way, we never calculated the cost of forgone wages, of the many hours in which Sean wasn't billing clients, of how many dollars he wasn't bringing in. Nor did we plan for the painful reality of the months that would drag on with no progress on our house because Sean was away working for customers.

Suddenly I had a maxed-out Home Depot credit card. And a Visa. And a home-equity line of credit. If money is the root of all couples' stress, then we had one giant taproot underneath our relationship. But we couldn't refinance the house and get out from under that ever-accelerating interest rate because we couldn't exactly have an appraiser walk in and look through the studs from the front door to the back door. We couldn't sell it because it wasn't worth what we'd invested, and we couldn't finish it because we didn't have the money. Meanwhile we fought, broke up, and got back together. I felt angry and helpless. The cobbler whose children never have any shoes, my mother joked. And I was losing my mind trying to keep us afloat.

We could have walked away. We wouldn't have been the first

couple to do it, even before the meltdown. But neither of us wanted to give up on a house that we'd invested blood, sweat, and a lot of tears into. So we kept finding a way to make it happen. We threw raves in a warehouse that Sean leased for his remodeling business, renting the space to promoters for $400 a pop, sometimes running an illegal bar out of the back—twenty-one and over only!—and using the proceeds to keep our life and house afloat. Weekends I spent cleaning the warehouse, sometimes with my mother, mopping up vomit and other fluids I don't care to remember out of the toilets and off the floors. These are the types of things you do when you're on the financial edge.

I remember driving through the newly gentrified neighborhood of Washington Park one Saturday evening at dusk, looking in the lit-up windows and watching the couples still playing one last game of volleyball in the park and wondering what it must be like to have such luxury, to have a life where you weren't always hustling to keep it together. I wanted, just for one night, to sit at their tables, even if, in reality, I would have hated the cage of their lives. I knew my life was all of my own doing, my own choices, but just for one night I wanted to know what it was to have a Saturday free of any obligations.

As you might imagine, this life was not sustainable. Something had to give, and it eventually did. We devised a plan to move to Brooklyn together, to start over. I would find a better-paying job there, and Sean would stay back and finish the house and prepare it for sale. On New Year's Eve 2006, in the soft glow of our favorite Italian restaurant, he asked me to marry him. I said yes.

Finally, it seemed the life inside those windows was coming my way.

◆　◆　◆

Six weeks after I got to Brooklyn he announced that he was leaving me for a mutual friend. He'd read Elizabeth Gilbert's *Eat, Pray, Love* and didn't want us to end up trapped in the life she described. I'm pretty certain I'm the only woman in America who has been dumped because of Elizabeth Gilbert. For a while I wanted to punch her in the face. I actually contemplated a rebuttal story or *Village Voice* column called "Drink, Fuck, Smoke," wherein I would detail my search for everything in the dive bars of New York City.

The worst of it, though, was that we weren't just breaking up; we actually had to get a divorce. Colorado is a common-law state, and we'd held ourselves as married in the eyes of the law. When I first started at *Westword*, I put Sean on my health insurance as a spouse, and we'd filed as married on our taxes, even though he hadn't yet asked and I'm not sure I would have said yes. So without ever having a wedding or even a ring, I needed a divorce.

Let's just say it didn't end well. It ended about as badly as it could. He didn't want to sell the house, and I couldn't make him—let alone force him to move out—because we were both on the title. Neither of us could afford to buy the other out. I was stuck. I was manic, scratching the walls of my mind trying to come up with another solution. Round and round my mind would go, always in the same feedback loop, no new answers. Either I could keep paying the mortgage indefinitely or lose the house to foreclosure.

For the longest time I refused to believe I had to let go, even when Stacy told me it was the only answer, the only way to move forward. I didn't believe it, even when the banks and lawyers told me I had no other way out. But to let go would be to fail, to admit defeat, to let Sean take every last thing from me—even my dignity. So I juggled it all—Denver mortgage, Brooklyn rent—for more than a year before I threw up my hands in defeat. I just couldn't fight anymore. I called the banks and begged them to foreclose. It was the only move, the only way to finally quit Sean. Still, it would mean being branded with a scarlet F for foreclosure. There are no words to describe how I felt having to make that decision. After all, nobody had duped us into the house. But I couldn't stay stuck in that life, paying for the past and trying to move forward to the future.

When a friend walked away from her house with no regrets, I was horrified.

How can you do it? I wondered. Didn't she feel guilty?

I wanted to know how she could be so dispassionate about it while I was so humiliated. But for her the house was a profit-and-loss statement. She had run the numbers and decided the investment no longer made sense. Just like a bank would do, she said. She didn't have any concerns about walking away and leaving the house for her neighbors to maintain or to become a blight if they couldn't. She needed to start over, to begin again without the albatross of the house around her neck. Whereas I carry the guilt to this day.

She and I are no different from the millions of people who lost their homes to foreclosure during the crisis. Each one of us has a deeply personal reason why we had to do it; some we can understand, others we see as irresponsible. But each person was just trying to do right by themselves and their families, to just get by. Some of us went in with open eyes and the best of intentions. Some of us were duped or taken advantage of. A few of us had fraudulent intentions. And some people made out, flipping homes and driving up the prices to the point where entire markets were unsustainable. There's a lot of blame to go around, from the banks down to our own individual bad choices.

Space and time has given me the ability to see my own culpability and to start to forgive Sean. I am thankful that we both have better lives, better spouses, deeper relationships. We were toxic and brutal with each other, inflicting the kind of emotional wounds that take years to heal. I've also had to learn to stop judging myself and forgive. Still, I would have never guessed that I'd end up married and living in Detroit, looking to do it all over again.

CHAPTER THREE

"I THINK YOU LIKE ME," Karl professed, grinning.

That was his pickup line, how he got the girl. I'm not sure whether it says more about him or me.

We were walking home together from a friend's birthday at the Bait & Tackle, our neighborhood bar, and we could still hear the sounds of laughter cutting through the deep July midnight. Karl had offered to escort me home, having just discovered that our apartments were a mere block from each other. I, however, had known that for a while. I'd been quietly admiring him since we'd met that spring. I knew he had two cats. I knew he commuted to work on his fixie Bianchi, one of those bike guys in the silly racing outfits my father would never understand. I knew he cut a nice figure, his tall, lanky frame crouched low over his bike as he whizzed through the streets. I knew my dog, Maddie, liked him. What I didn't know was what he thought about me.

My mind spun with how to respond.

I think you like me.

It hung in the air.

He could mean, *I think you like me, and I like you too.* Or perhaps, *I think you like me, and while that is sweet, I'm not interested.* Seriously, how is a girl supposed to react to such a declaration?

I opted for the very articulate and committed "Um, maybe?"

He leaned down and kissed me, confirming that his intentions were not of the friend variety. It was one of those butterflies-in-the-stomach kisses, the type you dream of and hope all kisses will be like. We were both startled but smiling, and then he invited me in.

I politely declined.

The backdrop of our romance was the tiny neighborhood of Red Hook, Brooklyn, which clings to the waterfront like a barnacle, a small seaside village in view of Manhattan but entirely separate from its scene and scrum. I arrived in the fall of 2007 just as my relationship with Sean was dissolving. Everyone told me not to go to Red Hook, that it was too remote, too dangerous. But the minute I stepped off the B61 bus, I was intoxicated by the sheer otherness of the place. It felt as if I was standing on the edge of nowhere. Van Brunt Street, the neighborhood's main drag, was empty of people that afternoon save for an old man in a stained wifebeater, sitting on a metal folding chair and watching me walk down the street. Seagulls trolled the skyline, their shrill calls creating the white noise of Red Hook. Sea cranes stood sentry at the mouth of the neighborhood, waiting to unload the container ships that drifted in and out of the Buttermilk Channel. Civil War–era warehouses squatted side-by-side with brownstone row houses as industry and residents forged an uneasy peace in this old shipping port.

I was immediately smitten with the quirks and oddities lurking around every corner. A collection of Betty Boop dolls was lovingly displayed in a bay window facing the street. Giant blow-up pumpkins filled an empty lot; come Christmas it would be redecorated with a crèche, and feral cats would use baby Jesus's cradle as a nest. Magic-hour light bathed the neighborhood in a rose-gold glow. The Rosa rugosa, those rose-like flowers that grow on windswept beaches and other inhospitable environments, were in full fiery bloom in the rocks and crags along the waterfront. I walked out on Valentino Pier, which juts like a fist into the bay, and sat under the watchful gaze of Lady Liberty, alone in a city of 8 million.

In one afternoon I felt the powerful tug of the place, the possibility of home, even though I didn't yet know a soul. It was my sixty-five-pound pit bull, Maddie, who made friends here first. Within weeks everyone seemed to know her, know her name, even if they didn't know me or mine. My first-floor apartment had deep windowsills, and she would sit on them while I was at work, looking lost and forlorn, beaming pathos to all who passed by. When my landlord, Lucy, or anyone else would try to talk to her, she would turn her face away, as if to say, *I couldn't possibly*. She wouldn't be distracted from her mission. Maddie knew that if she were patient, I would return and take her to Valentino Pier, where she would dive deep into the waves, to the bookstore, the salon, or even to Tini, the lovely wine bar that let me sneak her in, health codes be damned. She came with me everywhere.

Maddie and I had been inseparable since I found her in a blizzard on the streets of Denver four years earlier. A flash of movement against the white snow caught my eye out the window. I thought it was my neighbor's dog, Poquito, running through the storm, so I ran outside to grab him. Instead I found a tiny pup cowering in the doorway of the school next door. I named her Maddie—short for Madeleine L'Engle, my favorite author—and brought her inside. I already had a dog—a 120-pound Rottweiler named Nina—and three cats. I didn't need another pet. But when she looked at me with her big pleading eyes, I couldn't resist. I know now that she deploys those gazes very strategically.

It was Maddie who found Karl.

She and I were enjoying a late-afternoon Negra Modelo at the Bait & Tackle, where I'd become a regular in hopes of making some friends. Bait is the quintessential locals bar: dark and stuffed with larger-than-life characters. Taxidermy covers the walls, from the black bear in the corner to the geese stapled to the ceiling by their webbed feet. It's the kind of place where you earn your way in, do time on a barstool, before the locals give you the nod. They are looking for proof that you'll still be sitting there, one of them, when the tourists and rose-gold light of fall fade and the desolate bleak skies of February cocoon the waterfront.

I was reading a book in the corner when I noticed Karl sitting at the bar counter. Maddie was splayed out in front of the door, forcing everyone to pay her a love tax as they passed. I watched him for a minute and then got up and went outside to have a smoke. When I returned, she was sitting at his feet, staring up at him lovingly.

"I'm Karl," he said.

"That's Hot Karl," bellowed the bartender, a surly Irishman named Chris, not to be confused with the owner, a surly Irishman named Barry. The peanut gallery of regulars cackled at the joke I didn't understand.

All the regulars have a nickname. There's Steamer and Sniff, Captain Chris and Canadian Chris, Crazy Dave and Whiskey Dave. And Hot Karl, who wasn't so named for his good looks but as a reference to a sex act I'd rather not have had a bar full of grown men explaining to me.

I introduced myself and then Karl turned back to his beer. That was it. It wasn't exactly an instant romance.

We kept running into each other—it's hard not to in a small town—and I started up a casual flirtation. Maddie would flop at his feet given the chance, and he would rub her belly. I, however, got nowhere. Our conversations always seemed to falter; he always seemed a little distant or disinterested.

Apparently I wasn't direct enough. Karl later told me that he wasn't aware of my flirting. It wasn't until I made a profound fool of myself that he took notice. We were back at the bar—I swear we did things other than drink, Mom—making small talk while he monitored Eurocup on the television. I asked how he'd been, and Karl told me he'd been working out, trying to lose a little weight and get back on his bike. The winter had imposed a hiatus on his daily commute over the Brooklyn Bridge and into Lower Manhattan, where he worked as a software developer.

"I think you look tight," I said.

The worlds tumbled out of my mouth before I could stop them. I wanted to die, to melt into the floor, anything to get away unnoticed, to take it back.

He turned and looked at me.

"Thanks," he said. "That's sweet."

Then he turned back to the game.

And that was that. I'd done my best. I'd humiliated myself; my dog had thrown herself at him. He just wasn't interested. I was ready to give up.

Then a few weeks later, seemingly out of nowhere, he made his grand profession.

I think you like me.

I was completely caught off guard, but I know now that it was typical, wonderful Karl. He takes his time to process information, so long that you might think he has forgotten about you or the topic at hand. So long that sometimes you aren't sure whether he's listening at all. And then, when you least expect it, he speaks up with a proclamation or snippet of insight.

We had our first date that weekend. It was an all-Red-Hook extravaganza. We went to a book reading at Sunny's Bar and had drinks at Bait and pulled pork sliders at the newly opened Brooklyn Ice House, which would soon compete for Maddie's affection because the bartender, our friend Tammy, would feed her bacon as we passed. It's hard to compete with bacon.

After dinner Karl stepped away to the restroom. The bill came while he was gone, so I paid our $12 tab. I didn't think much of it because, well, I've paid for every first date I've ever been on. Talking about money makes me uncomfortable; seeming as if I don't have any money makes me even more uncomfortable. So when a bill presents itself, I strike preemptively, reaching for it first even when I'm about to max out my credit card or wipe out my bank account. But my small gesture, made out of habit and insecurity, touched Karl.

Nobody had ever paid for him before.

Nine months later we moved in together.

◆ ◆ ◆

Karl and I fell in love with Red Hook together. We both liked it individually, but as a couple, it became home. It is where we expanded our family when we found a giant Rottweiler abandoned in Coffey Park. Neither of us wanted another dog at the time, but when he rested his giant blockhead on Karl's shoulder as we drove him to the vet to be scanned for a microchip, I knew this bear cub of a dog would be ours. Karl named him Leroy and jokingly tries to blame him on me because I have a history of bringing in strays, but we both know the truth: Big Bad Leroy Brown is 100 percent Karl's dog.

We loved that it could take an hour just to walk a few blocks because we ran into all of our neighbors. We loved that we knew all of the small business owners and counted them among our closest friends. Karl volunteered at the Red Hook Community Farm, composting the coffee grounds he picked up daily from Fort Defiance. I organized free movies in the park during the summer and helped manage the neighborhood community-supported agriculture program. We loved that in the fall the owner of Fort Defiance, St. John, hosted a pig roast right on the street. We loved that his friends, Ben and Souhi, who ran the Good Fork restaurant down the street, helped him, as did Barry, who owned Bait. We loved that when a fire broke out at Home/Made, the community quickly raised thousands of dollars to help get the owners, Monica and Leisah, open again. We loved that real work and industry still happened here. We loved that it was a blue-collar town, not just a tourist district all prettied up for the guests.

But for all of that, it was still a hard neighborhood. Had always been a hard neighborhood. It had stabilized and was no longer ground zero for crack, mob hits, or the packs of wild dogs that had roved the waterfront less than a decade before. But the nearest subway was still a mile walk; the B61 bus was unreliable at best, and the laundromat was only open sporadically. The streets were rarely plowed, and sometimes you would be snowed in for days, the busses unable to traverse the routes. And the city regularly proposed building garbage-transfer stations in the tiny village, as if those who lived there were garbage themselves. You had to want to be here.

My first landlady, Lucy, only knew Red Hook as a place of abandonment and disinvestment, the place *Life* magazine once dubbed the "crack capital" of America, and the home of Brooklyn's largest public housing complex. Although glad to have me as a tenant, glad that new people were interested in her home, Lucy was confused by our appreciation for what she saw as a place she was stuck in, a place she never got out of.

"Aye, Amy, no. It's too dangerous," Lucy called to me as I passed by her on the stoop, off to walk Maddie in Coffey Park, just a half block from her four-story brick building.

She'd raised her four boys in Red Hook but never let them go to this park despite its basketball courts and shady maple, oak, and gingko trees. People lurked in those branches, she said, waiting to leap down and mug you. That was her Red Hook.

"No, Lucy," I told her. "It's not like that. There are people in the park, other people with dogs and kids. It's safe."

She looked at me quizzically.

But it was. By the time I arrived in 2007, the park was the beating heart of a neighborhood on the precipice of significant change. Red Hook was in the beautiful chaos, that moment when things aren't as dangerous as the bad old days but not so cleaned up and overdeveloped as they will become.

Karl and I couldn't imagine living anywhere else—and had fewer and fewer reasons to leave the neighborhood. I would venture out to other parts of Brooklyn when needed, but I avoided going to Manhattan other than for work. Almost nothing could pull me into its canyons. Relief washed over me every time I fled over the Brooklyn Bridge back to my own borough, elation every time I rounded the corner into the neighborhood and saw the giant Red Hook letters lit up on the side of a building, telling me I was home.

But as others began discovering our hidden shores, rents began to rise. As they always do. Shells of buildings were listed for a million bucks—buildings that might need at least another million in rehab costs—and found buyers. Small business owners who had opened when nobody wanted to be here—like Barry and Ben and Souhi and Monica and Leisah and all the rest—feared they'd be pushed out in favor of those with deeper pockets. Celebrity artists, not just working artists, moved in. The streets ran thick with tourists on bicycles.

Karl and I knew that if we wanted to stay, it was time to commit—perhaps past time. Our apartment was an amazing spread by any standard, with two bedrooms, two bathrooms, in-apartment laundry, and a private roof deck. This was unheard-of luxury in New York City and only affordable because we'd chosen to live on the fringes. But we knew if we were going to make Red Hook our permanent home, we'd need to buy a place. So we started looking and researching, trying to figure out what we could afford.

We discovered we'd missed the curve. There were very few apartments for sale, and we couldn't put 20 percent down on a million-dollar building and still afford the rehab. We lived a comfortable middle-class life, having money to eat out and travel on occasion, but that alone took a hefty income. Sure, we could have lived on less; many of our friends did and do. Many New Yorkers do. Many people everywhere do. My family certainly does.

But I was still carrying a lot of debt from my house in Denver, and honestly, I wanted to have the nice things I dreamed of as a kid. I wanted a nice apartment and the ability to buy a new pair of shoes without wondering whether my debit card would get declined. I was a long way from the days of getting by week to week with the help of pawnshops and payday lenders, but I wasn't rolling in it either.

Karl, however, comes from a few rungs higher on the class ladder than my family. He grew up comfortably in Tennessee, his dad an ophthalmologist. I'm the first in my family to go to college; he's the only sibling without a PhD. He was taught to be frugal, an excellent value that I too was taught . . . because we didn't have any money. There were no conversations in my household about what it means to come from poverty and enter the middle class. What is the protocol and etiquette for suddenly having nice things—and wanting them—without being offensive to those who don't?

I know it's hard to feel bad for a young, childless couple with good jobs. But if we couldn't make it, who could? What of our friends, who'd arrived in the 1980s and pioneered the changes that were now attracting developers and big money? What of our neighbors in the public housing? What would all of this change mean for them?

That's when we began fantasizing about where else we might live, mostly in the hazy, dreamy, not-at-all-real way that New Yorkers discuss other, less expensive locales with exotic names like Austin and Asheville. You talk about going, about that other life, but can't imagine actually leaving.

But even as Karl and I dreamed of a future together, we were also in the "are we–aren't we" phase of our relationship. We needed to either move forward or move apart. We'd broken up several times as we tried to merge two distinctly different personalities. I'm an ambitious type A, get-shit-done kind of girl. Karl, meanwhile, is perfectly happy to just enjoy life. He is typically satisfied, whereas I am always searching, unsettled. He can sit on a barstool and enjoy small talk with strangers for hours; small talk makes me want to stab my eyeballs out. He's an extrovert to my introvert. I'm fight. He's flight.

Like my father, I have a temper that flares quick and hot but fades almost immediately; Karl is more like my mother, for whom raised voices, any fighting, wounds the soul. My weapon is controlling the argument and bullying Karl until he feels like he can't say or do anything right and has few words at his disposal. He goes silent and walks away, which just infuriates me further. Learning how to engage in spirited disagreement, especially when each of us felt like our very nature was under attack, was hard.

It didn't help that I was feeling adrift in my career. All the ideals that had brought me to journalism—the power of storytelling, the possibilities for standing up on behalf of the disenfranchised and telling the truths behind corporate and political spin—were slowly being strangled under the weight of day-to-day demands. Office politics, page views, BuzzFeed, social media, marketing, selling, producing content—none of it was about journalism. What about the lofty goals I had as a kid reading Henrik Ibsen's *Enemy of the People* or, later, *The Reconstruction of a Racist*? What would the high school student I'd once been, newly empowered and impassioned by journalism, think of the career she'd built? Was I speaking enough truth to power or just building a comfortable life as I rose up the media ladder?

So when I was accepted into the Knight-Wallace Fellowship at the University of Michigan in Ann Arbor, it felt like a life raft. Almost since the beginning of my career I'd dreamed of being accomplished enough to earn a spot. Still, I never expected to get the call asking me to come. I'll never forget when it did come— 6:52 a.m. on April 30, 2012—because I knew the moment I hung up the phone with the director that my life was about to veer into a wholly unknown direction. I didn't know where this would take me, but I knew there was no way a paid year off to study, think, and travel wouldn't change who I was. It's like winning Willy Wonka's golden ticket of adulthood.

The question was: Would Karl come? He told me to do whatever was right for me. He didn't want to influence my decision to stay or go. He meant to be respectful and loving, but to me it seemed like he didn't care what the outcome would mean for us as a couple. I needed to know whether he envisioned a life with me. Ever since Fruita I'd sworn I would never give up my future for a man, but here I was, at thirty-seven, with one failed relationship behind me and thinking about what I wanted going forward. Karl couldn't answer whether he would quit his job and his life to come with me. He also didn't know whether we could survive a long-distance relationship or if we should break up. If he wouldn't go with me, would I stay? If I did, would I always think of him as the man who made me choose between career and love? I was unsure of how to move forward or even how to stand still. But Karl needed time to choose.

Karl finally gave me his answer one evening two months later while we were watching an episode of *Battlestar Galactica*. I'd just returned home from a weekend apartment-hunting trip in Ann Arbor with my best friend, Stacy. While there, she and I had a few wine-fueled dinners, during which we attempted to grok the beast that is Karl. Stacy had a few theories. Stacy Cowley *always* has a few theories. (Some of them are crazy theories, like the one where Wyoming doesn't really exist—it's just a wild government plot. But we love her all the more for them. Even my dad is charmed by his other daughter, though he just shakes his head.) Today's theory was that Karl didn't know if he should come to Ann Arbor because he wasn't sure whether I wanted him to. I hadn't told him I was committed, that I was in. We were both waiting for the other to blink, to go first. We were both afraid to tell the other we wanted to be together, maybe even get married. One of us was going to have to profess first, so if I wanted him to choose me, I was going to have to cowboy up and choose him.

I pressed pause on *Battlestar Galactica* and said, basically in one long breath, "Stacy Cowley has a theory. She says you want to come, that you want to marry me, but that you are scared to ask me because I haven't told you I want you to come. Are you scared? Why don't you want to marry me? What is wrong with me? Don't you love me?"

Karl looked at me, a little uncertain, perhaps a little terrified.

"Well," he said, "I've been thinking about it. I think we should get married. If I'm going to move across the country to be with you, I think that means we're ready."

He paused.

"Will you marry me?"

"No."

"No?"

"Now I think I bullied you into asking me instead of you really wanting to marry me," I replied. "And we've been drinking. You have to ask me again in the morning so I know it's real."

"Okay."

He pushed the play button, *Battlestar Galactica* resumed, and that was that. He asked again in the morning, and I said yes.

We started planning a big Red Hook wedding with all of our friends and family. We dreamed of vows on Valentino Pier, with the same seagulls and ships that first drew me here. We wanted a pig roast out on Van Brunt Street, a big rollicking street party with everyone invited, a celebration not just of us but of our community and home.

But as we faced our looming move, that wedding became too overwhelming to plan. The logistics would be a nightmare. How would we bring in family and friends from Colorado and Tennessee on such short notice? How would we pay for it and also a move? How would we pack the house, relocate our lives, and get married all in less than three months? We were paralyzed just thinking about it all.

Ultimately we just snuck off and got married at Brooklyn Borough Hall. I didn't even buy a gown; I wore the same royal blue cocktail dress I'd bought for our engagement party. We didn't tell our families, not even Stacy, until it was over. I wanted her to be there, to stand beside me after more than a decade of friendship, but I didn't want to ask her to take another day off of work. She'd just taken off several consecutive Fridays to help me pack and house hunt in Ann Arbor.

When Stacy called, I knew I was in trouble.

"Hi," I answered sheepishly.

"Your mother called. She would like to know if you just got married."

That morning I'd posted a photograph of my wedding flowers on Facebook along with a sign from Fort Defiance wishing us well. That had unleashed a torrent of confused calls to Stacy when I didn't answer my phone.

"Surprise?" I said.

"Hmmmm."

"It was an impulse," I tell her. "I didn't want to ask you to take another day off work."

"Really, after a decade of friendship you think I'm not going to take off one more vacation day to see my best friend get married? Nobody at CNNMoney would have stopped me."

I couldn't argue with her. The facts were cold and hard and on her side. But to my mind the wedding was just a formality, paperwork to make the move easier. We would do the "real" wedding when we returned and had time to plan and invite everyone. That would be our real anniversary, the date of our real marriage. This was just the trial run. We were already committed and living together. How different could things be after a ceremony at City Hall?

But as we had stood at the altar in the nondescript courtroom, the judge saying our vows so quickly we would later joke that we had no idea what we'd promised, something inside me shifted. I cannot say what had changed when I said "I do," but the act of getting married made me feel different—safe, chosen. As someone who had never valued marriage and had been treating it as if it were simply a legal transaction, this was a completely unsettling and unexpected sensation.

To celebrate our nuptials we invited a handful of our closest friends out to the Far Rockaways for a night at Boatel, a flotilla of abandoned yachts that artists restored and now rented out for $50 a night. Goats wandered around the docks, and the website warned that "though we aim to be hospitable, remember that you are joining us in the rough + tumble and please come adventure ready."

Our "honeymoon suite" was the Sweet Annisa, which I can only describe as 1980s-era coke-lord den, complete with gold-framed mirrors just waiting for guests to cut a few lines. I tried not to touch the bedding and faux-fur pillows strewn about the cabin, convinced that they were infested with bed bugs. I covered everything with the blankets and sleeping bag I had packed and hoped for the best.

"Congratulations, you two!" toasted Stacy as we walked out on deck. She was standing on the dock and holding up a bottle of Buffalo Trace, surrounded by our friends who were dressed, inexplicably, in costumes—pink wigs, Mexican wrestling masks, sparkly dresses, and life preservers. Rich, the chef in the group, was manning the grill, and burgers and steaks added a smoky pungency to the salty sea air.

"We found them in the cabin of our boat!" yelled Maddie, who was in the pink wig.

James hugged me as I climbed over the bow and then helped Maddie and Leroy onto the swaying dock. Overhead a thin veil of stars covered us. Usually the city's light pollution overpowers them, but out here on the fringes, where sand and sea kiss, I could almost make out the vastness overhead.

"We love you, Lovey!" called Cristina, evoking my nickname for Karl.

Someone cued up our song, "Right Down the Line" by Gerry Rafferty, on the stereo, and I grabbed Karl for our first dance as a married couple. I laid my head on his shoulder, and we swayed to the music, trying to keep our balance on the dock and not fall off into the oily waters below.

CHAPTER FOUR

"BACKYARD IS UNDERWATER."

The texts started rolling in rapid-fire, ping after ping after ping.

"Landlord said we may lose the chickens. The coop is only a few feet high."

"We are peaking at about 20 inches of water."

"Bar is flooded; water is three feet high. Lost everything."

"No power is expected for weeks. Generators are running, but gas is short."

Just two months after Karl and I left Brooklyn for Ann Arbor, Hurricane Sandy, known locally as That Bitch, slammed into the East Coast and sent sixteen-foot waves crashing onto Red Hook's shores. She crept silently up the streets, submerging cars and, yes, even chickens. Homes and businesses were flooded, with the crest markers hitting six feet on some walls. Our friends would be without power for months and without homes for longer; insurance companies would withhold desperately needed checks; politicians would bloviate endlessly.

The morning after the surge Karl flew into action, packing the car with generators and submersion pumps—items desperately needed for cleanup but maddeningly unavailable in the tri-state area—and drove home to Brooklyn. What he found were our people, our community, resilient as ever. But they were shell-shocked. So many whose finances were tenuous to start with now faced rebuilding with no resources. Hundreds of volunteers flooded into the neighborhood, delivering food and supplies and mucking out basements. A roving bar cart delivered cocktails and levity on the street. They were dark days, buoyed by spirit.

Meanwhile I was six hundred miles away, warm and dry, with an epic case of survivor's guilt blooming. I organized meetings with the power company and set up Kickstarter fundraisers to help people get back in business. But no matter how much I did, I knew it would never be enough. Red Hook would forever be changed, and those who lived through it would be bonded in a community of survivors. There would always be an emotional demarcation line, as clear as the flood line staining the walls, of life pre-Sandy and life post-Sandy. It felt like the end of an era as the Red Hook we knew and loved rolled out with the receding tides.

On the morning Karl and I had left Red Hook for Ann Arbor, we'd driven past Fort Defiance, where we had spent so many mornings and evenings lingering over coffee and cocktails, and saw that someone had written us a farewell message on the chalkboard sign outside: "Good luck and safe travels, Karl + Amy. You will be missed." I remember pressing my forehead to the window, trying to hold back the tears that were welling up. I was positive we would return. I told everyone to hold down the Fort, that this was just an extended honeymoon.

But now I wasn't so sure. How would we reintegrate into this tight community, not having experienced what they had? With dogs and pianos and our life, we needed a first-floor apartment, something we now feared. For me Sandy was the beginning of a psychic shift away from Red Hook, a letting go. It would be a long and painful process, just like the end of any intense love affair. There is the moment you know, even if it's just a fleeting glimpse. Then there is the rejection of that knowledge. Then finally the acceptance, the moments of doubt, and finally letting go. Sandy's aftermath was that first moment for me, enough to open my heart to the idea of other places, other opportunities.

What I did know, however, was that our future did not lie in Ann Arbor.

We had arrived there on a warm, late August afternoon, all a little road weary. It's only a ten-hour drive from New York, an easy stretch for a truck driver's daughter, but this had been an exhausting trip, with our knees crunched into the dashboard of our aging Saab hatchback as two dogs, two cats, four suitcases, and one vacuum cleaner all jostled us two humans for space. Even Leroy's indefatigable spirit was fatigued. Still, when we pulled up to the curb and saw our new house, we had to sit and stare for an extra moment. Three stories, yellow, with a deep front porch.

We'd rented the house off Craigslist sight unseen, so we hadn't been sure what to expect. We'd initially hoped to take a small furnished apartment, just enough to get by. We wanted to store our stuff in Brooklyn and travel light. But landlords didn't like the idea of renting to out-of-towners when they had a market full of easy candidates, especially not out-of-towners with two cats, a Rottweiler, and a pit bull. Once, we were turned down in favor of a dozen undergrads. We got so desperate that we contemplated buying a house and then renting it out when we left. But that seemed extreme. So when this one appeared on Craigslist, saying it was pet-friendly and showing photos of a fireplace and beautiful wood trim, I e-mailed immediately with a note I hoped would convince the owner to take a risk.

"Dear beautiful house," it began. "We would love to live in you, at least based on your photos. You see, we are moving to Ann Arbor from Brooklyn, where we live in an amazing apartment with a roof deck, but we've always dreamed of having a porch like yours. If you have lilacs, we would probably marry you . . . "

It was silly, but it worked. And now the house in the photos that I'd seen online were staring back at me. Definitely not a Craigslist scam. Thank god!

"Holy crap, Lovey!" I called down to Karl as I walked up the stairs to the third floor. "You won't believe it. I found another room. This place goes on forever!"

Our landlady, Diana, laughed when I told her that. To her, the house is just your typical three-bedroom home with just one bath, a real deficit for most tenants. But to us, the three-thousand square feet seemed palatial.

"I should only rent to people from New York from now on," Diana replied, only half joking.

I immediately began making plans to hang fuchsia plants around the porch, the same frilly pink-and-white ones that my mother always had, and find two rocking chairs so we could enjoy cocktail hour outdoors in this strange new Michigan world. Late summer, no humidity, perfectly manicured lawns fronting perfectly maintained homes—we certainly weren't in Brooklyn anymore.

I whipsawed between profound loss and profound excitement.

When Karl and I woke up the next morning, we were excited to go in search of our new Fort Defiance and get our morning coffee: black for Karl, latte with three sugars for me. But we soon discovered there wasn't a café anywhere in our neighborhood; the nearest option was a chain—and we'd have to drive to get there.

"How do you drive if you haven't even had coffee yet?" Karl asked, puzzled. Nearly twenty years of dense urban places had left him unprepared for the vast spaces and strip malls of suburban towns. Every morning in Red Hook we would stumble downstairs to Fort Defiance for our morning coffee. It was a ritual that was less about the caffeine than about the connection and conversation we found with our neighbors.

We quickly added "buy coffee maker" to our to-do list.

That morning was a harbinger of how intensely out of place we would feel in Ann Arbor. Although many famous and brilliant people have called its streets home, from Ken Burns to Bob Seger to the CEO of Craigslist, we never really connected. Its rhythms weren't ours. We were too old to fit in with the college kids and too young for the people our age, in that we're not burdened with the responsibilities of children. All vestiges of the counterculture hippie town Ann Arbor had once been were long gone. Instead, the town felt bland and overpriced, cloistered by its own intellect and affluence. The closest thing we could find to a regular hangout was the gay bar where the food was good and the people welcoming. But we didn't really belong there either.

"Quit complaining, kid," Dad said when I tried to explain our sense of alienation. "You're not seeing the opportunity here. You can always have fun tormenting the yuppies."

Dad. Ever the optimist.

Instead, the house became our haven, our buffer against a world we didn't understand. We chose to think of this time together as a prolonged honeymoon, an opportunity to explore what it meant to be married without the obligations and intrusions of the "real life" we left behind in New York. In Red Hook we had an entire community to rely on; we didn't really need each other. But here, disconnected from everyone, we would need to find strength in one another.

The first few weeks were particularly intense. I hadn't yet started my program, so Karl and I were together constantly. In Brooklyn, thanks to busy work and personal schedules, we were guaranteed to have time and space apart, something we both need and cherish. I could guarantee Karl would be out of the house a few nights a week so I could decompress and read a book or indulge in my guilty pleasure "stories," as my friend Cris likes to call them: *Veronica Mars, Sons of Anarchy, Vampire Dairies*. But in Ann Arbor Karl was always around and underfoot. We'd go out exploring by ourselves—him biking through town, me walking Maddie in the arboretum—but still our unstructured days seemed to stretch out before us, unending. We found ourselves staring at each other and wondering what else there was to talk about. In retrospect it sounds delightful to have that time off together to live and explore and think, to revel in the luxury of time. But it's always easier to appreciate something when you no longer have it. In the thick of it, with the future a black tunnel before us, I felt knotted with anxiety and frustration.

I felt so much pressure to make everything easy and perfect for

Karl because I'd convinced him to give up everything he knew to follow me, something I wasn't sure I would ever have done for him. I'd brought him to this strange new place where we couldn't even walk down the street to get a cup of coffee. I wondered whether I'd ruined his life, our life. But I also didn't want to burden Karl with my doubts. I didn't even want to admit that I had doubts. I didn't want to look weak. I wanted to be strong and supportive, to help him thrive and have a meaningful experience, not just be the tagalong spouse in the program.

But then there he would be, in my space.

I reached the edge of my patience one afternoon while unpacking the house.

"Why would you put that there?" I yelled at him, exasperated.

He was putting dinner plates away in the cabinet I'd reserved for the drinking glasses. Everyone knows glasses go in the cupboard next to the sink. Why didn't he? We'd already squabbled over where to put the baking pans, the silverware, and even the spices, and yet he insisted on being in the kitchen.

"Can you go unpack the rest of the house?" I snapped at him.

Half-open boxes were piled everywhere, and bubble wrap floated across the floor like loose dryer sheets.

"But what if . . . "

I winged a granola bar at him. It narrowly missed his head.

It was like I was having an out-of-body experience. I could see myself picking the bar up, as if in slow motion. I could see that it was chocolate chip, my favorite; he prefers peanut butter. I could see all of this, but I was powerless to stop the toss.

I've just thrown a granola bar at my husband.

Karl looked at me, unsure of what just happened. Then he started to laugh, breaking the tension that had been building up for days.

Karl is always laughing. It's how he expresses happiness, how he conquers stress. He laughs at everything. Sometimes it annoys me because we have such different senses of humor. I often don't understand the joke or think he's laughing at me. But on that day I was deeply thankful for his love of the absurd.

I put down the breakables and tried to explain how I was feeling. He seemed so miserable here, I told him, and I feel like it's my fault. I am scared that he blames me. I'm afraid that I don't deserve to be in the fellowship, that I'm not as good or as smart as the other fellows. I've read their bios, and they all seem so accomplished. I'm afraid that I'm going to be a terrible wife. I don't know what I'm supposed to do or how to act now that there are rings on my finger. Is it supposed to be different?

Karl hasn't asked anything from me, but I'd placed all of this pressure on myself to be this perfect woman with dinner made and house cleaned. Like somehow I was supposed to be my mother even though my mother doesn't want me to be her. I wondered whether Karl was silently judging me and asking why he married me. I'd spun myself into an emotional death spiral thanks to all of the uncertainty, all of the newness, each question begetting more questions and insecurity.

"It's okay, Lovey," he said. "We're both really stressed out."

He confessed that he too is suffering from anxiety and insecurity. He is worried about whether he can live up to Stacy, who he knows is the first person I call about everything. He's concerned he won't be enough for me here because he's not a journalist. He's afraid he won't fit into my world, won't fit into the fellowship, and that nobody will like him. He's afraid he's going to be lonely and left behind. What if he wasn't enough, wasn't a good enough husband? What if I wished I hadn't married him? But he didn't want to tell me, to burden me.

I just want to kiss this man.

"But everyone loves you, Karl!" I exclaimed, hugging him, all of the rage of a few minutes ago dissipated. "You're Lovey!"

My girlfriends will remind me of this in the coming months and years whenever I'm frustrated with him for some small infraction. *Remember when you threw a granola bar at your husband . . . and he thought it was funny?*

This marriage stuff is hard.

◆ ◆ ◆

As I was trying to embark on my own marriage with Karl, to start my future, my parents' marriage was falling apart.

After we left Fruita, Mom and Dad started a small excavating company, Bear Excavating and Construction, with all those scraps he collected from Maco. They slowly grew it into his full-time job, then my mother's and eventually my brother's. But small business life is hell, and those years of struggle took a toll on my mother. There's no time off, no time away. She felt more like an employee than a wife, while my Dad felt alone trying to keep it all together. When the recession hit in 2008 and work dried up, it just exposed the fractures.

The timing couldn't have been worse. All of their sacrifice and hustle was finally starting to pay off. There was money in the bank and a positive balance sheet. Bear was poised to grow, for success to finally be had, but now there was nowhere for Matt and Dad to go. Their fleet of trucks and tractors, the grown-up version of my childhood Tonka trucks, sat unmoving in the red Colorado dust. My father paced the house like a caged animal while my mother, after a lifetime of raising kids and managing Bear's office, had to go "back" to work. At nearly sixty years old, she was running the floor of a JCPenney for $9 an hour. As the resources dwindled, my brother and his family had to move in with my parents and claim unemployment benefits. Fruita repeated for another generation.

It all just got too hard for my mother. My dad was too hard. Life was too hard. Everything was just too damned hard. So after thirty years together, she filed for divorce.

When they told me they were getting a divorce, it wasn't exactly a surprise: part of the reason Karl and I eloped was that I could not face my own vows while watching theirs start to crumble. I didn't want to spend my wedding day worrying about them, alternating between vicious anger and heart-stopping sorrow over the collapse of my family. It was so much easier to not tell anyone, to run off and keep them at bay, two thousand miles away.

But once it was real, I lashed out like a teenager. I wanted my mommy. I wanted my daddy. I hated them both. I wanted to protect them both. I never wanted to see either of them again. I silently berated them because their split meant Karl would never experience a Haimerl Family Christmas. I recognize that in the scope of a divorce, Christmas morning is not a high concern, but the traditions are so central to how I grew up that it felt like Karl would never get to fully understand me. I didn't miss a Christmas at home until I turned thirty-four.

Dad always planned a scavenger hunt for Christmas morning, and I wanted Karl to enjoy one. I wanted him to walk upstairs with me and my brother's family, not a minute before 6 a.m. by my mom's edict, and see the tree. Each year we would go and cut one together and then decorate it. I wanted him to know that the first thing you do is scan the tree to see whose name is written on the outside of a creamy linen envelope. That person would be the lucky hunter. My first pair of cowboy boots, fire engine red, came to me this way.

Dad would send us all over the house searching for the clues, which he wrote out in his own leaning script. Sometimes his hints and rhymes were so obtuse that it would be hours before the hunt was over. But that was the point—he made Christmas fun even when there was very little under the tree. It didn't really matter what was at the end of the game either; it was about the process. We would always break at some point for my mom's homemade cinnamon rolls, which filled the house with the scent of brown sugar and cinnamon while the Christmas morning casserole sent out competing hints of hot sausage and spicy eggs.

But my husband would never understand Christmas because my parents stole it. He would never understand that what had started out of necessity and innovation had become something so much more to me: a joyful ritual signifying that our family could get through anything together.

Karl tried to be supportive and help me through the emotional turmoil. He'd been through it with his own family and understood what it is to be the adult child of divorcing parents, to feel like you have to be fair and balanced, not take sides, even as you work through your own anger and sadness because what's happening to them is happening to you too. It's tough at first, but it gets better, he promised.

I tried to be an impartial listener, though only my father really spoke to me. My mother distanced herself from me, saying she didn't want to burden her children. Fair. But as a result, my father and I drew closer together while my mother, a woman I once spoke to every day, became a shadow figure in my life. It was heartbreaking and confusing. I was stuck wondering what it means when the man who bought you, who called you his own when the first one didn't want you, is no longer wanted. Would he still want me? Would I still be his daughter? My father, it turns out, had the same fears. He was terrified I wouldn't want him in my life anymore, that I would choose my mother and abandon him. He was afraid he would lose more than just his wife as his entire life cleaved apart.

"I will always be your daughter, Dad," I told him. "Nothing will ever change that."

And he would need his daughter more than ever to get through the coming months and years. He wasn't just losing his wife; he was losing his business and livelihood. Running Bear Excavating required three people: my mom, my dad, and my brother. It probably should have been me running the office instead of my mom; maybe then things would have been easier on my family and my parents would still be married. But instead they sent me off to college, to be the first to get out, while the three of them struggled to build and grow.

But as their marriage collapsed, the whole couldn't stand. The love and the fight was gone. My dad gave up. My brother was lost. And my mom didn't know what to do. So Dad finally said, *Shut it all down, sell it all*. Everything he worked for, every shred of his identity, would go to the auction yard. Ashes to ashes, dust to dust, tractors to auction. RIP Bear Excavating and Construction.

In December 2012—four months after leaving Red Hook and two months after Hurricane Sandy—I flew to Denver to help sell off Bear at the Ritchie Bros. winter equipment sale. I couldn't do much to help physically, but I wanted to be there to support my brother, Matt. I would do anything for him. When I was nine years old, I sat on the tailgate of the old Ford and wished on a shooting star for him. I promised the universe that if I ever got a little brother, I would be his staunch ally and forever protector; I'd be the kind of sister Meg was to Charles Wallace in *A Wrinkle in Time*.

On the morning of the auction Dad gave me a pair of his Carhartt overalls. He knew how the cold prairie winds could rip you open as you stood out on the flat open expanse of the Ritchie Bros. lot. He'd stood there many times himself, buying tractors, slowly building up Bear. Now he was selling it all back. I slipped on a knit cap and prepared to face facts.

My father couldn't bear to watch "the vultures" feast on his bones, so it was just Matt and me there to sell off everything he had ever known or worked on, every dream for his future. Meanwhile my mother would watch the events unfold from afar. She too was losing everything she'd worked and fought for, but she wasn't wanted here. This was something Dad and Matt had to do together, but they needed me onsite to get them through it.

We didn't expect much, just pennies on the dollar, because the market was flooded with the heavy yellow iron that so many men like my dad had had to unload before him. Auctions were brisk as the recession killed small business after small business. Despite all the talking heads saying the economy was coming back, that the Great Recession of 2008 was over, nobody in my family's line of work was feeling it. One friend of Dad's, unable to face losing his wife and his livelihood as his business collapsed, took his own life. Matt and I worried that our father might be harboring similar feelings, and we kept a hushed suicide watch.

After Dad dropped me off outside the gates, I walked in and found Matt inside the cab of his service truck, going over the final details. He left the Bear name painted on all of our equipment, so he was easy to spot among the long rows of identical-looking machines. Most sellers don't leave on their company decals, but we wanted everyone to know they were buying Bear: quality machines loved and mechaniced by Dick and Matt Haimerl.

Matt hugged me, and we desperately held on to each other until there was nothing left to do but wait. I told him I would sit inside the auction shed and keep track of sale prices and call with updates.

First, though, I needed to visit the D2s, the two tiny bulldozers that started Bear. I was with Dad when he'd bought them many years before at an auction not so dissimilar to this one. That was at the beginning, and now I was at the end. Fat tears spilled down my face, but I did not care, even as people looked on with sympathy and uncertainty. I let out a gut-wrenching scream that wracked my entire being as I mourned what was and what could have been, knowing that everything from here on out would be different. There would be no going back. I was a woman without a home.

The auctioneer's call started, and the first dozer rolled.

◆ ◆ ◆

My plan for my fellowship year had been to study what I titled in my application "America's Abandoned People and Places." Even I was a little vague on what, exactly, that meant. I wrote that "I liked dying places and hard-luck cases—decaying southern cities, desolate Western bust towns, and abandoned manufacturing hubs. Even more, I love the spirit of the people in these places. I'm eternally fascinated by their lives and their choices. But when the jobs are disappearing, how do you create new ones? How do you raise kids, build homes, and feed your family in places that have become economic cast-offs? I believe the stories of these places and people are missing from our public dialogue. We use them as props in articles about the 'jobs issue' or 'manufacturing' or 'poverty,' but rarely are they more than quick sketches to prove a point rather than they themselves being the point. Who is watching out for them?"

Watching my father's life disintegrate made me realize that what I was really seeking answers to were questions plaguing my own family. Why am I rising, why am I succeeding, while they fall further behind? What makes me special or worthy? I'm no better than them, no smarter, no more anything. My brother has a degree in diesel mechanics, while I have a degree in making the words pretty. In case of a zombie apocalypse, I know which one of us I want on my side. But here I was, at a fancy fellowship, getting paid more than my dad has ever taken home to ask these questions.

I needed to understand how that was fair. How could the world forget about the men and women like my brother and parents who have to work so hard for so long with so little respect? I wanted to understand why they seem to just be pawns on the chessboard of politics and corporate greed, their lives misunderstood and mischaracterized at best, ignored at worst.

At the start of the fellowship I'd made color-coded maps of the country as I tried to identify the perfect storm of poverty, unemployment, and migration. I thought I could find my answers in data and economic indicators. But now I knew I had to look inward, into my own heart. I had to make peace with who I was and where I came from as part of my search for answers. I had to find a way to move forward and build a future and a home with my husband, even as everything I'd known and relied upon crumbled beneath me. I had to let him inside, to go easy on him, as Dad would say, to tenderly figure out our life together.

Initially I clung to the dream of Red Hook because of the stability it represented, even though I knew in reality that we couldn't go back. We'd always be renters there, succumbing to the trail of gentrification marching ever deeper into Brooklyn. Our dream wasn't New York City at any cost; it was Red Hook specific. And the Red Hook that lived in our hearts and minds was gone. No amount of wishing was going to change those facts.

But where we would go, I didn't know.

I thought maybe it was time to travel and explore. Try out a few cities, see what stuck. I took the Foreign Service exam, imagining that a life overseas might be the thing for us. But when I found out I'd passed and could move forward in the process, Karl confessed a secret dream: he wanted to own a home. He desperately wanted to be somewhere permanent, a place we could commit to and build a life. He was tired of feeling transient. Karl's confession came as a surprise. I thought he'd want to travel, to try places on before committing. That's his temperament: he's cautious and analytical, incredibly risk averse. He loves station wagons. I had thought he only wanted to buy in Brooklyn as a way to arrest time, to preserve his tiny claim to the waterfront. I hadn't thought the actual act of ownership mattered to him, certainly not ownership of a single-family home. He'd never shown any signs of domestication, never craved a yard or honey-do lists. But after twenty years negotiating shared space, living with the sounds and smells of neighbors on all four sides, he was ready for something that was his, to plant gardens and paint walls without asking permission.

He looked over at me, hopeful and pleading.

"I want to do it in Detroit," he quietly said.

He wanted to be a part of rebuilding Detroit and letting it build us. We'd talked about Detroit, of course. The city had been a siren calling to us on so many of those late nights spent romanticizing a life outside New York. But those fantasies were based on the hazy remnants of a trip I'd made to Detroit once before, almost a decade earlier, on vacation with Stacy. We'd picked Detroit because it was centrally located between her in New York and me in Denver. I wanted to see the Diego Rivera murals at the Detroit Institute of Arts, and she wanted to explore the halls of the famed John King Books, four floors of dusty volumes. Nobody had told us tourism was dead in the D. We were stopped at the border, after an evening in Windsor, because the agents couldn't believe we would vacation in Detroit. They actually laughed at us. Still, that was when the city, with its mash-up of grit and glory, started its slow roll into my heart, offering itself as a plan B should I ever need a plan B. And here Karl and I were, needing a plan B.

Based on that one weekend I expected to fall in love with Detroit, madly, passionately, and immediately. I'd read about all the tech firms opening and artists flocking to the city, heard that it was the next zeitgeist. The next Brooklyn. You could buy a house for nothing and live cheaply; there was nothing but empty land and possibility. Billionaire Dan Gilbert was being heralded for reigniting downtown after relocating his mortgage-origination company, Quicken Loans, and seventeen hundred employees to Detroit. It was a boomtown, and the tagline was *Opportunity Detroit*. Kid Rock told everyone so in his Super Bowl ads. Detroit: the intersection of muscle and brains.

I imagined Detroit as Red Hook writ large. I knew there would be blight and disinvestment; I'd read the stories and seen the photographs. But I was not prepared for the devastation and poverty Karl and I saw on our first visit to the city together.

We'd come just before the fellowship started in search of a grand

piano so Karl could spend his year studying jazz. He'd spotted one
on Craigslist that we decided to go check out, using it as an opportunity to visit Detroit. But as we drove toward the shop on Detroit's
far east side, I wondered where in the hell we were. Literally, maybe,
hell? We could see where Detroit morphs into the wealthy Grosse
Pointe suburbs, the have-nots crashing right into the haves at the
border. On one side is where Old Money lives in America, the kind
of money that bankers on Wall Street dream of having. On the other,
charred remains of low-slung buildings lined the street. Some were
haphazardly boarded up, if they were sealed at all. The occasional
check-cashing store, tire shop, or chicken joint broke up the devastation. Chained dogs guarded the storefronts. The summer sun beat
down on the pavement, hot and malicious. I felt open and exposed in
the way many people do when they visit Colorado, the big western
skies bearing down on them with nowhere to hide.

This isn't the Detroit we'd been hearing so much about. This
didn't look like the "Comeback Kid." Where were all the artists and
entrepreneurs supposedly flocking to the city? Where were all the
companies that are relocating? Where was anyone? The street was
empty except for a man coming out of the Alabama-Style Chicken
and Fish down the street.

"Should we lock the car?" Karl asked, uncertain.

We normally don't. We never leave anything of value inside,
and we don't want a broken window to be the cost of someone
finding out.

"I don't know. I don't want it to get stolen."

We didn't know what was normal or even how to act normal.

I thought I was prepared. I thought I was ready for the blight and
abandonment and everything we'd heard about, read about, and been

told about. But while ruin and disinvestment can look picturesque, like potential, when it's contained within one square mile of cobblestone streets running along a scenic waterfront, it's another thing entirely sprawled out across 139 square miles. Nothing matched the emotional reality of standing there and seeing it in person. It was like the first time I saw Georgia O'Keeffe paintings in a museum. I'd never cared for her work before that; it just seemed like flat pictures of flowers. But when I stood before her *Bella Donna* at the museum in Santa Fe, I was overcome. I could see the layers, the depth, the beauty, and the pain. It was overwhelming. Detroit felt like that, like something photography and words had flattened, couldn't capture, and I was now experiencing all of its depth, beauty, and pain. Still, I couldn't comprehend or contextualize everything we'd seen. I had no idea whether it was indicative of the city as a whole or if we were just seeing a small and particularly ugly pocket. Was Detroit worse than we had imagined?

I thought things had to be better in downtown and Midtown, the heart of the city's economic resurgence, where Detroit was supposedly thriving. That's where Gilbert was on a buying spree, collecting Detroit's art deco skyscrapers like trading cards. But even there the city looked raw. Party stores and empty lots lined the blocks, while the skeletons of abandoned buildings lorded over the skyline. Most of the storefronts on Woodward Avenue, the city's main drag, were empty. A few construction cranes were flying—signs, my mother would say, of good things to come. Development brings cranes, cranes bring jobs, and jobs feed families. Any time she sees a crane, she's thankful somebody has work.

It was hard to discern whether the talk of Motown's return was real or imagined.

Karl, however, wasn't deterred by that first trip. Despite what we'd seen, he still felt like this city would be home. He can't say how he knew it; he just did, in the same way he'd known I was the one. And the feeling got stronger for him each time he visited, which he often did while I was traveling or otherwise engaged with the fellowship. He liked those hours alone with the city because we explore so differently. He enjoys getting lost, seeing where the road takes him. I like a direction, a plan. If we're going to get lost, I want that to have been the plan.

He began to bring me to the city, showing me its softer side, gently encouraging me to fall for Detroit the way he was falling. The more we came, the more I started seeing all of the beauty that is hiding here in plain sight. I fell in love with the giant sculpture of Joe Louis's fist, punching south toward Canada, that is inexplicably but awesomely installed at the intersection of Woodward and Jefferson Avenues. The two spines of the city connect at the fist. Hart Plaza was breathtaking as we walked through the sculptures, fountains, and monuments, looking out at the waterfront and watching the freighters plying the Detroit River. A nearby plaque reminded us that this was once a crossing on the Underground Railroad. There is so much history here, so much quiet splendor, but you miss it all in a car. That's the story of Detroit: it might be the Motor City, but you don't understand it, feel it, see it, until you walk it.

We enjoyed sitting outside 1515 Broadway Café and watching the People Mover pass by. Detroiters may deride it as a "toy train" to nowhere because the elevated tram only loops around downtown, but sitting there, watching it pass, the trees in bloom and the street streaming with people, I could almost imagine I was sitting in Paris. When I visited with Stacy these blocks were empty; now more than eighty-five thousand people work downtown and thirty-five thousand residents call it home.

Karl and I toured the Eastern Market, hunting the city's best street art. I've been a passionate aficionado of graffiti since college, when I taught computers to so-called at-risk urban youth. I taught them Photoshop, and they instructed me in the differences between tagging and graffiti. They gave me the language of street art, which is useful here in Detroit, where it is everywhere. Some of it is shitty tagging—scribbling with spray paint, essentially—but then you come around a corner and see a mural that stops you or makes you laugh or makes you think. The work is constantly evolving, but a few personal favorites are already emerging. There's Kobe Solomon's Chimera, a winged lion that spans nearly nine thousand square feet and silently watches over Detroit; Malt's stylized owls on the Lincoln Street Art Park; and Katie Craig's vivid waterfall of colors that tumbles down the side of a nine-story building in New Center.

Each new mural, new place we uncovered, the more our first experience on the far east side receded, becoming just one part of the story. We don't forget, never forget, that Detroit, but there was also something compelling about this complicated town. We thought we might want to be a part of it even while recognizing that there would be some difficult questions ahead about race and class and who gets to live here and who is a Detroiter. I wondered whether I would even have the right language for the conversations. After all, the closest thing I had to an experience that might prepare me for living in a minority-majority city was my short time in Jackson. Would we be welcome, or would be just be seen as white gentrifiers?

Am I really ready for Detroit? I wondered as Karl made his confession. He believed. He felt the connection and commitment to this place. He wanted to be a part of whatever was happening, even if we didn't quite know or understand what it was yet.

As the fellowship neared its conclusion, I received job offers in Detroit and in Oakland, California. When the company brought us out to Oakland for me to interview, I was immediately drawn to the sea cranes dotting the harbor. Oakland felt like Red Hook but with more sunshine. Plus, there was a giant dog park on the water, amazing food, and the chance to lead my own publication. Karl, however, was Team Detroit. He was the devil on my shoulder as we toured the better city by the bay.

Honey, he said, *with the cost of living here, we might as well stay in Brooklyn. Lovey*, he pleaded, *this place is beautiful, but I don't feel connected the way I do in Detroit.*

And then the kicker: both papers were offering me the same salary. In Oakland, he said, you will be the editor-in-chief and have all the responsibility, but we'll struggle financially because of the housing costs. In Detroit, for the same money, you'll be a reporter. You'll have time, he offered, to do freelance, enjoy your life, take a break after years of hustling harder. Or at least try some side hustles.

But sunshine, I countered! Good Mexican food! But, but, but . . .

Back and forth we went as the sky faded to dusk and we switched from day drinking to evening cocktails. I stepped outside the bar into the soft, warm California night to smoke a cigarette and think. I could hear the buoy bells echo across the water.

"Hey!" a group of bros hollered at me as they walked up the street. "It's not safe for you to be out here by yourself. You need some help?"

There was no edge to their voices, but they started sidling uncomfortably close. My instincts told me they posed no real harm, that they were most likely a group of San Francisco tech boys out slumming it, proving how brave they were by being in Oakland for an evening.

"I'm fine," I called to them. "Just smoking a cigarette." I'm tough, after all. I'm my father's daughter. I'm missing a knuckle on my left hand from a barroom brawl, and I own a pit bull and a Rottweiler. (Nobody has to know I was breaking up the fight and that my dogs are marshmallows.)

"Don't you know this is Oakland?" asked the tall one, who was wearing a Raiders jersey. "You could get murdered, and nobody would even notice."

"I'm from Detroit."

They stopped in their tracks.

"Oh shit, you got this. Wow. What's it like there?"

"Fucking fantastic."

Decision made. In that split second I had called on the street cred of a city I couldn't even call home yet. I hadn't said New York or Brooklyn or even the Bronx. My first instinct revealed to me what my heart wanted: Detroit.

CHAPTER
FIVE

I'D LIKE TO SAY IT WAS FATE that my husband and I found the house on Van Dyke Place, that it was our one and only, that we'd seen no others before her. I like the romanticism of that. Or I'd like to say that we looked at dozens of homes, that we scoured every neighborhood in Detroit before finding ourselves standing before a house that's biggest assets seem to be a tomcat and streetlight. I like the pragmatism of that, that we would be those kind of people, ones who research and calculate before jumping. But in reality we came to this house through pure serendipity and chance. And that, we've learned, is the Detroit way.

Karl and I were exactly as naive as you might suspect when we first started house hunting in Detroit. We weren't even considering renting because we'd read all the stories about the $500, $1,000, and

$10,000 houses. The prices felt like Monopoly money: we could buy a house for less than our *monthly* rent in Brooklyn. We thought we'd find a cheap house, fix it up, and live large.

It's a wonder that our real estate agent didn't smack us upside the head.

But Ryan Cooley has been there, done that. He runs O'Connor Real Estate and Development, while his brother, Phil, is more famous as the model-turned-entrepreneur who opened Slows Bar-B-Q, Detroit's temple to decently good brisket that everyone from the *New York Times* to *Food and Wine* has raved about. The real estate agency and Slows sit on the same stretch of Michigan Avenue, the pothole-riddled six-lane artery that bisects Corktown, the hipster haven of Detroit. This block is often the first place newcomers discover, drawn not just to the BBQ and real estate but also to the pour-overs at Astro Coffee, craft cocktails at the Sugar House, and stiff drinks at LJ's Lounge. This is an abnormal block, a place where locals bring outsiders to show off the city's best side—or at least the side most likely to look like any urban experience they've previously had—in hopes of enticing them to come.

Walking toward Ryan's office, Astro coffee in hand, I can see him through his window as he talks with a couple. Ryan is slight in stature, dark hair, slightly graying, but with a youthful appearance. You can see in the way he carries himself that perhaps he's always been overshadowed by his brother's good looks—though he too is handsome—and has turned inward. It makes him a thoughtful, patient, articulate guide through the vagaries of Detroit real estate and living. I can almost imagine the conversation he is having with the couple standing beside him:

No, a $1,000 house doesn't come with a working bathroom.

No, definitely not a kitchen.

No, the houses you read about aren't move-in ready. They need a lot of work.

No. You don't want a $1 house. There is a reason why it's a buck, even in Detroit.

And he has answered those questions often. It was early 2013, and people like us had heard about the cheap houses in Detroit and were clamoring to get in.

"I'm dealing with a lot of people who are moving here because they want to move here," Ryan told me. "And that kind of demand, well, I've never had it in the eight years I've been doing real estate."

But then, as now, there weren't enough homes to go around, despite more than eighty thousand abandoned-looking properties dotting the landscape. Most require extensive renovations that would cost more than the house would be worth when completed. Those that were move-in ready—meaning basic power, heat, and water—were often priced too high for the low expectations of bargain hunters. Whenever Ryan lists a house that is in good condition at a good price in a good neighborhood, it disappears. All cash offers. Deals made in a day. Even homes in the wealthy Indian Village neighborhood, with their ballrooms and carriage houses, can sell in a day, for cash, at prices that push the $300,000 barrier, which is expensive in a city where the median sales price is less than $20,000.

It's the great irony of Detroit: the city is drowning in properties, yet it can be impossible to find a viable home to buy.

But Ryan was ready to help us find one. He asked us what neighborhoods we were interested in and what level of renovation. Cosmetic updates are fine, we tell him, possibly a kitchen or bathroom renovation, but no gut renovations. And being isolated in Ann Arbor, we want to be somewhere close to the city center or in Southwest Detroit, somewhere we can walk to get a cup of coffee in the morning and meet our neighbors on the streets. We would consider other neighborhoods if they fit that description, but we don't have a good mental map of the city yet and don't know where else those might be. Detroit is so large and sprawling—you can fit Manhattan, Boston, and San Francisco inside the city's 139 square miles—that it can be hard to get a real sense of the geography. We know the city center is where most of the reinvestment is happening and that Southwest Detroit is thriving thanks to a growing Latino and Arab population. But the further you radiate from the city center, the worse the conditions and the rarer the strong, stable neighborhood still holding on in the face of the blight. I think of Detroit as a slice of Swiss cheese: each hole represents an intact neighborhood, while the cheese is the distances you have to traverse to find them.

We considered some of the historic areas such as Boston-Edison and Palmer Park, which feature gracious, tree-lined blocks and the types of mansions and prices that make you drool, but the areas felt too remote. There was no density, nothing to walk to. The commercial districts that once served these communities had long since shuttered or were filled with the types of services that prey on the weakest among us, from check-cashing shops to rent-to-own furniture stores. And even here, so many homes were abandoned. It was unsettling as we drove between these neighborhoods, some of the strongest and most stable in the city. The "cheese" between them was blight and abandonment— entire blocks had become ghosts of the lives once lived there.

The suburbs, we told Ryan, weren't an option either, though friends and strangers tried to convince us we should move there rather than the city proper. You should go where you'll be safe, they told us. Where there are streetlights and garbage pickup. Where the same house can be worth $500,000 on the suburban side of the street and less than $100,000 on the Detroit side. We heard the refrains everywhere. Sensational media reports warned us. My punk rock hair stylist in Ann Arbor cautioned me. Seatmates on planes told me in hushed tones that I should be careful, even though they just told me they lived in Detroit.

Oh, they would say, *you mean you're moving to the actual city?*

Won't you be scared?

You will get mugged.

Don't stop for gas.

Trust no one.

As embarrassing as it is to confess now, the constant barrage of ill will got to me. It made me scared. It made me doubt our decision. Who wouldn't, given Detroit's reputation? There were times driving through the city at night, the streetlights dark, when I imagined bad intentions lurking in every vacant lot, behind every overgrown bush. I wondered whether I was safe anywhere in the city. Would I get mugged just getting out of my car? There is rampant poverty—40 percent of the city's residents live below the poverty line—and with that comes the desperation of people just trying to survive, whether by stealing, scrapping, or slinging. In a forgotten place there are most definitely forgotten people. To deny their struggles would be naive and disrespectful. But the stories made it sound like Detroit wasn't safe anywhere, like it was one of our postapocalyptic TV shows but without the actual apocalypse.

Still, the suburbs were never even an option. They may be lovely, but Novi, Birmingham, Royal Oak, and all the others could be any suburb of any city anywhere in the country. There is nothing special, on a grander scale, to them. They are missing, as the southerners would say, a sense of place. But Detroit, Detroit has identity and soul. It shapes you, evolves you, challenges you, moves you. For us, the suburbs simply offer a comfortable, bland backdrop for living your life.

And yes, I feel like an asshole just saying this. After all, when Patti Smith moved to Detroit to be with her husband, Fred "Sonic" Smith of the band MC5, they moved to the tiny suburb of St. Clair Shores to the northeast of the city. Ain't nobody more punk rock, more city, more authentic than Patti Smith, so who am I to judge? Nobody, other than to judge what is right for my life.

So I make no bones about my strong distaste for the suburbs. Not just of Detroit but of anywhere. I don't like them, never have, never will. I don't begrudge anyone who lives there. Do what works for you and go with God. But for me, it's cities or small towns, which in my experience are one and the same. Cities organize themselves around functioning small towns where everyone knows your name; it's how you make the massiveness, the unknowable, human. Cities offer all the benefits of small town life plus the cultural and life amenities that come with millions of people living in one place. Suburbs, conversely, feel as if they are created to ensure maximum anonymity, from the chains that populate the strip malls to the attached garages.

And oh how my father hated those garages.

When we left Fruita, my parents packed up everything and headed to Denver and the jobs in its booming suburbs. We couldn't have been more out of place, but the rent was affordable and the schools were good, and my parents weren't sure yet where they wanted to land. Dad hated it, especially those damned attached garages dotting our cul-de-sac. They reminded him of everything he never wanted for his life. He hated watching people glide into their garages night after night, the gaping maws swallowing them as they steered their

Camrys and Astrovans inside. The door would slowly roll down, shutting them away, allowing them to go from the personal bubble of their car directly into the personal bubble of their house without ever having to come into contact with another human, without ever having to leave the comfort of their own identity and worldview even for as long as a conversation. The garages were monsters that ate your soul, took your empathy, and left you disconnected from the greater world around you. They were the downfall of humanity.

Or maybe they were just places where you park your car.

But you can see how I might have been indoctrinated against the suburbs from the jump.

It was Detroit or nothing.

◆ ◆ ◆

"Look," said Karl, calling me over.

He pushed his hand through a hole in the wall.

We were standing in a fire-damaged Victorian duplex, the first stop on our two-home tour of what was available and met our criteria in Detroit at the time.

"A drug hole," said Ryan.

Dealers used it to pass merchandise and money back and forth between the two units. Somehow this charming detail hadn't made it onto the sales flier. Then again, there were no sales fliers. The house, which needed a complete renovation, was being auctioned off to anyone who wanted it for $8,000. As I looked around, I could not even fathom the rehab costs. Still, it had good bones and was in the heart of Southwest Detroit, the best food neighborhood in the city. Tacos galore, tamales everywhere, plus shwarma and kebabs and that garlic fluff, toum, that may be the condiment of the gods. We could walk to everything and be part of a thriving community. That, along with the turrets and built-in bookshelves, was nearly enough to seal the deal for me. Karl and Ryan, however, were dubious. Making the house fit for human habitation was a significantly larger project than we had told Ryan we wanted.

The next house was a Mediterranean-style mansion with a clay tile roof and curb appeal. An abandoned lot gone to seed was the neighbor in one direction, once-grand homes converted to eldercare facilities in every other direction. The house was gorgeous and only $24,000, but it too was a giant restoration project. Plus, the neighborhood lacked toum or any other food to speak of. It felt like a dead zone.

We passed on both.

Patience, we told ourselves. *Our house will come.*

Detroiters suggested we wait for the Wayne County tax auctions, when bidders can score homes for as little as $500. Each year the county seizes properties for failure to pay back property taxes. Thousands of homes hit the auction block, but you can't inspect them before you buy, and the horror stories are enough to arrest even the sturdiest heart. There are stories of houses that were stripped and slashed and defecated in. There are houses with tenants who refused to leave. There are houses with floors that collapse as the new owners walk through the door. And then there's the possibility that you are buying a house that belongs to someone whose life took a terrible turn for the worst and they just hadn't been able to pay Detroit's sky-high property taxes in three years. You moving in means they find themselves displaced and homeless. No. That wasn't for us. If we were going to walk into a wreck, we wanted to do it with our eyes wide open and without anyone to evict.

Ryan told us he'd call when something new came on the market.

Serendipity intervened instead.

She first introduced herself in the guise of April Boyle, a stunning woman with long, dark hair punctuated by a bold streak of white blonde cascading down her face. We met her at Cliff Bell's, a downtown jazz joint where her organization, D:hive Detroit, was hosting its monthly panel discussion on small business issues in Detroit. As the new entrepreneurship editor at *Crain's Detroit Business*, I decided to attend, thinking it might be a useful way to start getting to know my new hometown.

When Karl and I walked into the club's art deco splendor, we were almost immediately engaged in conversation with local business owners and wannabe shopkeepers about what was happening in the city and our planned move. But even in this pro-Detroit crowd, we found ourselves repeatedly answering the ever-popular, ever-lingering question: Why?

Honestly, we couldn't articulate it yet. We maybe didn't yet know. All we knew was that we were ready for something, looking for something, yearning for something. But what and why Detroit? Well, that was still more in our hearts than in our heads. The best we could come up with, the truest answer we had—and the one we still have—is the people. They have something, a southern hospitality mixed with a wry knowing, grit and compassion and exuberance all wrapped together. It's not a reason to buy a house in Detroit in the economic analysis, but it's every reason to buy a house in the emotional analysis of what makes a home and community.

When April came over and introduced herself, she said she'd heard we were moving to Detroit.

Yes, yes, we are, we replied excitedly, prepared to have the "why" conversation again. I explained that we were house hunting and made a joke about the lack of houses in a city that is swimming in them. She offered a knowing laugh.

"I think I might know of one," she said. "It's not on the market yet, but I can put you in touch with the owners. It's across the street from my brother-in-law."

Serendipity.

The next day I am armed with a phone number for the couple selling a house in the West Village, a neighborhood we vaguely know but had never really considered. We've heard that some friends from Red Hook are opening a coffee shop there, though, so it seemed promising.

For being a journalist, I have a real hatred of phones. If it's for work, I can pick one up and call, but for personal business I practically have a phobia. I make Karl call for things like reservations because I hate making first contact by phone that much. I e-mail, I text, I tweet, I Facebook and Instagram, but phones . . . unless you are my husband, my mom, my dad, my brother, or my two closest friends, it probably ain't happening.

Instead, I took the chicken's way out: I searched for the owner on Facebook.

Bingo!

I crafted a nice message expressing interest in the house and explaining how I'd come to hear about it. I hit send and then realized, *Shit, that just went into the "other" mailbox, the place where Facebook messages go to die.* If you are friends with someone, a message turns up in their main inbox; if you're not, you go to the "other" purgatory where the message is practically guaranteed to remain unfound. Unless you pay a dollar. Then Facebook will send your message directly into the recipient's inbox.

I ponied up a buck and sent it again. Within the hour I was on the phone with Alyson, chatting away like old friends. She and her partner, Fatima, live in Boulder, Colorado, and purchased the house a year earlier, hoping to get job transfers that would bring them home to Detroit. When I tell Alyson I grew up in Colorado and went to high school in Golden, just twenty miles south of Boulder, we swap stories and laugh at the serendipity.

They hate to part with the house, Alyson tells me, having wrested it away from a Florida slumlord, but they couldn't rehab it from afar, and their job relocations are looking increasingly unlikely. They haven't yet put the house on the market because they don't want to sell to just anyone. They are searching for owners they believe will fulfill their promise to the neighbors: to build a home out of the last vacant house on one of Detroit's most coveted blocks.

She gave me the address and lockbox code and told me to go see whether we feel what they felt. We agreed to talk again the next day.

So here I am, speaking to a 1914 Georgian Revival on a blustery spring day, being politely grilled by my future neighbor who happens to be the brother-in-law of the glamorous woman from Cliff Bell's and friends with our real estate agent.

Detroit is one small town.

◆ ◆ ◆

For two weeks Karl and I waffle over buying the house, poring over our finances and trying to figure out exactly what level of stupidity this decision hits: minor inconvenience or outright bank-busting craziness. The asking price is just $35,000, which seems reasonable given that Alyson and Fatima cleaned up all the back property taxes and other issues when they pried the place away from the previous owner. But the renovation costs are daunting. They've given us their plans and cost estimates, and they expect it will take nearly $150,000 just to get the house livable, which doesn't include kitchen appliances or even new windows. We could do it if we break into our 401(k)s, but it feels risky to bet our retirement on a house in Detroit. Plus, I don't want to pay the hefty taxes and penalties the IRS charges for early withdrawal.

I'd like to get a mortgage, but I know it's almost impossible here in Detroit. In 2013 just 10 percent of homes were bought with a mortgage. And it's not because of bad credit or tight lending: homes simply aren't worth anything in the eyes of banks and appraisers. Houses have been selling for so little for so long that when appraisers try to pull comparable sales to establish what a property is worth, they can only find severely depressed values. It doesn't matter that a buyer and seller have agreed on a deal; the banks won't finance it because they only see an overvalued property. So if you want to buy, you likely have to come with financing of the cold and hard variety. Still, I hope that if we pay cash for the house, we can get a construction loan for the rest.

We sit on our porch in Ann Arbor, rocking in our rocking chairs, sipping coffee, debating, and flip-flopping.

Karl loves the house and wants it; I don't want the financial risk. Besides, it has no front porch.

I love the house and want it; Karl doesn't want the financial risk. Besides, it has no front porch.

"Maybe," I suggest, "we should rent first, just to be sure we want to live in Detroit long term."

After all, we are talking about a pretty serious investment in a city we barely know, in a neighborhood we've visited fewer than a half-dozen times, and in a house that doesn't meet any of our initial criteria. It has no front porch. It's a full-gut rehab. And although there are rumors of new restaurants and cafés opening, they are just that—rumors. But we're not the first couple to stare down the barrel of this decision. This isn't *Star Trek*; we're not "boldly going where no man has gone before." Seven hundred thousand people still live here, build their lives here, for better and for worse. We're simply moving to a city that's down on its luck; we're not joining the Peace Corps or embarking on a humanitarian mission. Plus, if we manage to stay married and not kill each other, we'll have a fabulous home for a fraction of what our friends in Brooklyn pay in rent for their apartments.

But what if it all goes entirely wrong? I cannot even fathom that.

Round and round we go until, finally, Alyson and Fatima call and force us to decide. They have another offer. They want to sell to us, but if we're not serious, they need to move forward.

Karl and I look at each other, remembering that backyard, that streetlight, that white cat on the roof.

I'm terrified. I never expected to find myself here again, looking at buying and rehabbing another house. Even though we were house hunting, it didn't feel real. But now that we're agreeing to move forward, I am anxious and nauseous. My body remembers, even as my brain tries to forget, what it is like to have the constant stress of money and unfinished projects hanging over your head like a piano just waiting to fall. I don't want that to ruin Karl and me the way it did Sean and me.

But neither do I want my fears, the sins of my past, to prevent my kind and loving husband from enjoying his dreams. I know how much this place means to Karl. And I love the way he believes that this giant mess of a house can one day be a home for us. He believes in me. He believes in our future. And I believe in him.

Clear eyes, full hearts, can't lose.

◆ ◆ ◆

Buying a house in Detroit is actually easy if you're paying in cash. You don't even need a lawyer. In fact, we negotiate our deal over Skype, Karl and I huddled around our laptop while Alyson and Fatima huddle around theirs, all of our dogs making appearances during the negotiations. It's a simple transaction—no mortgage, no contract riders, no appraisals, no nothing. After all, what would any of those things tell us that we don't already know? That we're batshit crazy? Got it. That we're buying a collapsing house in a collapsing city? So we've been told. It's nothing we haven't already told ourselves.

What you don't do is just write the sellers a check. You use a title company to execute the sale and make sure everything is on the up-and-up. They will alert you if there are any liens on the property or back taxes you weren't aware of and insure you against any future ownership claims. Title search is standard in any real estate transaction, but it is the security blanket of cash deals.

The night before Karl and I are scheduled to close on the house, I have my first home-renovation dream: Karl perishes in a fire and I'm left to deal with the house and the renovations alone. I wake up spooked, aware that my first concern was not that my husband was dead but that I would face this project on my own. I am naturally hesitant to share this with Karl.

That afternoon we drive into the deepest suburbs of Detroit to the offices of the title company. We get lost, driving around an office park of identical buildings with no discernible addresses or identifying marks. Thankfully we ate before we left because, in our relationship, this type of unknown situation, coupled with hunger, is always the recipe for a giant fight. For some reason it always happens to us while driving through New Jersey, and this neighborhood looks and feels to us a bit like New Jersey. We are wary.

Eventually we find both the building and the office and are escorted into a nondescript beige conference room. We sign a number of forms, write out a check, and we are done. They don't even hand us a set of keys for symbolism. The set in the lockbox hanging on the door to the house is now ours.

Where to celebrate? We start driving back toward the city and realize we don't know our new hometown well enough to know where we should go to mark the occasion. We'd love to go somewhere in our new neighborhood, but the only option is a buffet at the Big Boy. We consider something fancy and historic, like the London Chop House or the Whitney, but we are now $35,000 poorer and have no idea how much worse it will get.

We find ourselves instinctively navigating our way toward the house. Yes. That seems right. Celebrate on the steps of our new home. We stop at the party store around the corner and buy a bottle of Woodford Reserve bourbon, the coating of dust on it signaling that this particular brand isn't a big seller here—this is more of a Crown and Beefeater joint. We don't have any glasses to clink with, so Karl adds two electric pink plastic shot glasses to our purchase.

We sit on our stoop and toast our new neighborhood, our new house, our new life. Then Karl tips out a bit of bourbon on the stone steps and christens our new home "Matilda," after the Tom Waits song "Waltzing Matilda."

I don't understand the connection. The lyrics don't seem to say anything about home renovation or Detroit or anything remotely relevant to my mind. But they express a lot to Karl.

"I have always had the sense that Matilda is this stately old dame who's come on rough times but can still be sort of cheered up," he says. "There's something very nostalgic about the song. You have the feeling that Waits understands immensely the things we go through in life. Like the huge amount of work and worry we're about to devote to this house."

Chin chin. To Matilda.

We pack up our impromptu picnic and head back to Ann Arbor, counting the days until we are reunited with our house.

When we arrive home, an e-mail is waiting in my inbox: "I had a dream about the house on Friday night after we signed the papers," Alyson writes. "All of us, plus lots of friends, were wandering through it. It was like a big 'pre-renovation' showing with lots of people and cocktails and mingling. I think it was a good-bye party (for us) and a welcoming party for you. And it felt really connected and right and celebratory and not sad for us at all."

CHAPTER SIX

NEWS FLASH. Standard & Poor's downgrades Detroit's debt to CCC-with a negative outlook.

I text Stacy: Detroit just got downgraded. We're now nine levels below investment grade. We just bought a house here. Whoopeee!

She replies: *headdeskbang*

One week after Karl and I bought Matilda and wed our futures to this city, the bond-rating companies are reminding us exactly how unworthy of investment they find Detroit.

Five weeks later the city will declare bankruptcy.

The city's newly appointed emergency manager, Kevyn Orr, will tell the world that the Motor City is broke, busted, $18 billion in the hole. In a black-and-white report he will list the city's many, many challenges: nearly 40 percent of the city lives in poverty, and the median household income is less than $30,000 per year; fewer than 15 percent of murder cases are solved, and police response time for priority-one calls—the oh-holy-hell-some-serious-shit-is-going-down calls—is 31 minutes in the best parts of the city and 115 minutes in the worst; half the city's residents—1.1 million people—have fled over the past six decades; the city has one of the state's lowest per-capita income levels and the highest per-capita tax burden. Add to this that nearly half of the city's streetlights fail to sputter on each evening; at least eighty thousand structures sit blighted and abandoned; entire neighborhoods have reverted to prairie; and ruin-porn tourism is a booming industry, as visitors from New York to the Netherlands flock to the city and gawk at the pain and devastation symbolized by such collapsing hulks as the Packard Plant and Michigan Central Station.

It wasn't always this way in Detroit.

In 1892 the city listed forty-two millionaires and would become exhibit A for the roaring twenties. Henry Ford and his four-wheeled revolution helped spread the wealth wide as he brought jobs to the great Motor City. When he announced his $5 a day wage in 1914, people flocked here, migrating from the South and further abroad for the unheard-of pay. Detroit was suddenly bursting at the seams, expanding to accommodate all of the newcomers and their new ideas. In one decade, between 1910 and 1920, the city doubled in population to nearly a million people. Developers saw this great boom and started pressing the city ever farther out from its core along the Detroit waterfront. Most of the homes in Indian Village and the West Village—including Matilda—were built during this time. Some developers with a build-it-and-they-will-come mentality pushed even farther outward. In 1921 the area of Brightmoor, for example, was platted an unheard of 12 miles northwest of downtown, with developers assuming the city would eventually annex the area and tie the new homes—built for migrants—to the city grids. They were right. The city grew from approximately 29 square miles at the turn of the century to 139 square miles by 1926.

It was a time of opulence and decadence as the newly flush auto barons and wealthy manufacturing executives attempted to one-up each other with new skyscrapers and public works. Today Detroit has nearly three hundred listings on the National Register of Historic Places, each a testament to how much wealth was flowing through the city. Union Trust, for example, built the Guardian Building as its headquarters in 1929, the structure rising forty stories into the air. But if the orange brick-, tile-, and terracotta-patterned façade is impressive, its interior is what inspires. As you walk into the building, it almost seems as if you've entered an art deco cathedral. The ceilings of the 150-foot-long lobby soar three stories and are covered in vibrant tile work in an Aztec design. The columns are made of Travertine marble imported from Italy and black marble from Belgium. This building shames Rockefeller Center, and it is the first place I take visitors because it is a visual reminder of what's hidden beneath all the stories of blight and ruin in Detroit.

In 1929 the Great Depression ripped across this city just as it did the country. Poverty. Despair. What started as a Wall Street problem quickly became a Detroit problem as demand for cars dried up, causing production to fall 75 percent by 1931. The automakers that had fueled the boom disgorged workers. Unemployed Ford employees and others staged a hunger march, which Henry Ford and police broke up with bullets. Grand old mansions were converted into boarding houses as people tried to scrape by. But for the wealthy, the good times continued to roll. *Life* magazine sent photographers to capture images of the extravagant masquerade balls hosted by the city's exclusive arts organi-zation, the Scarab Club. The Detroit Public Library opened its glistening white marble main branch, thanks to the largesse of Andrew Carne-gie, while the Detroit Institute of Arts built its now-iconic Beaux-Arts building across the street. Diego Rivera and his wife, Frida Kahlo, were the talk of Detroit when they came in 1932 so Diego could paint his infamous *Detroit Industry* frescoes in the museum courtyard. The 1930s ushered in the era of the labor unions, such as the United Auto Workers, and bloody battles as workers and the carmakers clashed violently over demands for better treatment and pay. In the 1940s the city became the Arsenal of Democracy as the automakers churned out tanks, planes, and bullets for the war effort. More jobs, more people, more wealth—more, more, more. The second great migration would start, and the city would hit its peak population of 1.8 million during the 1950s census as southerners, black and white, made their way north. This was truly a boomtown. Dan Gilbert's marketing slogan for the city—*Opportunity Detroit*—could have been the tagline then too.

But what good fortune giveth, it can taketh away—and nowhere knows that better than Detroit.

The automakers and manufacturers that led the growth of Detroit were also the sharp spear of its decline. They looked toward sub-urban frontiers, where they could build new, modern factories. As they left in the 1930s and 1940s, so did the jobs and the people, who followed their jobs ever farther away from Detroit. As the automak-ers churned out more cars and our soldiers came home from World War II, the automobile culture itself made ex-urban living feasible and desirable for more Americans whose livelihoods weren't tied to building cars. By the 1960 census the city saw the first of what would become six consecutive decades of population loss.

But Detroit's black population, which grew from just fifty-seven hundred people in 1910 to more than three hundred thousand in 1950, couldn't follow the white population in chasing the jobs outside city limits. They weren't welcome in those communities, even as the US government threw its full weight behind the postwar American Dream of suburban home ownership by guaranteeing home loans. In 1934, as the country came out of the Great Depression and foreclosure crisis, the feds created the Federal Housing Administration with the goal of increasing homeownership and spreading the payments and risk over a greater period of time. Before that, most mortgages were for three or five years, with a balloon payment due at the end. But FHA introduced America to the idea of the thirty-year fixed mortgage, guaranteed by Uncle Sam himself. Unless you were black.

FHA used a four-tier system of appraising neighborhoods, each with its own color code. Those well-to-do white neighborhoods were marked blue and were eligible for underwriting. Those areas that black families called home were "red," or danger zones, and were not. Matilda herself was redlined.

"If a neighborhood is to retain stability it is necessary that properties shall continue to be occupied by the same social and racial classes," according to the FHA Underwriting Manual of 1936. "A change in social or racial occupancy generally leads to instability and a reduction in values."

And if too many African American families somehow scraped together the cash to buy into a "blue lined" neighborhood—presuming black ownership wasn't against the area's covenants to begin with, as it frequently was—FHA evaluators could change the map and turn the area red, meaning nobody, black or white, could then get a federally insured mortgage there. White families could turn to banks and take on a high-priced mortgage—if banks were willing to lend in a newly "undesirable" neighborhood. Black families, however, were not eligible for most bank loans. Their only recourse was to turn to hard-money lenders, those who charge usurious rates in the hope that the borrower defaults, or to land contracts, where the buyer pays the owner on installment for the property, similar to rent-to-own schemes.

"Occasionally, FHA decisions were particularly bizarre and capricious," wrote Kenneth T. Jackson in *Crabgrass Frontier*, his seminal book on the suburbanization of America. "In the late 1930s, for example, as Detroit grew outward, white families began to settle near a black enclave adjacent to Eight Mile Road. By the 1940s the blacks were surrounded, but neither they nor the whites could get FHA insurance because of the proximity of an 'inharmonious' racial group. So in 1941 an enterprising white developer built a concrete wall between the white and black areas. The FHA appraisers then took another look and approved mortgages on the white properties."

These policies kept Detroit's black families trapped in neighborhoods such as Paradise Valley and Black Bottom—so named by French settlers for the rich, dark soil—which had developed into thriving enclaves boasting their own lawyers, doctors, and even hospitals. These areas also became centers of nightlife and jazz, blues and the Motown sound. But as the population swelled and the housing stock aged, the communities became more and more ghettoized. Those with jobs, with access to wealth, looked to leave, to find a better life for their families. But with federal housing policies subsidizing white and suburban development rather than urban improvements, those with little access to credit had little chance to escape. So while whites were accumulating wealth in the way most of us know how—buying a house and building for the future—black families were essentially shut out of the growth opportunities real estate investment provides, including the tax benefits of ownership.

"Black people were viewed as a contagion," Ta-Nehisi Coates put it in his article "The Case for Reparations" in the June 2014 issue of *The Atlantic.* "Redlining went beyond FHA-backed loans and spread to the entire mortgage industry, which was already rife with racism, excluding black people from most legitimate means of obtaining a mortgage. . . . Whites looking to achieve the American dream could rely on a legitimate credit system backed by the government. Blacks were herded into the sights of unscrupulous lenders who took them for money and for sport."

So despite the story that is often told about the roots of Detroit's current crisis, it did not start with the riots of 1967 that saw black families fighting back against increasing discrimination in every aspect of their lives. No, capital flight—or, what I like to call green flight—then white flight and eventually even black flight started long before the rebellion that flared into violence on the fateful night of July 23, 1967. The riots merely expedited the exodus already in progress of white and, eventually, black people out of the city. Families of white friends tell me they feel like they were forced out, that they were no longer welcome in the city. That it wasn't safe for them after 1967. They often cite former Detroit mayor Coleman A. Young's famous speech telling people to hit the road—Eight Mile Road—and get out of town. They tell me Detroit's first black mayor wanted them gone and that, for the sake of their children, they had no other choice. But they are only remembering part of what Young actually said: "I issue a warning to all those pushers, to all rip-off artists, to all muggers: It's time to leave Detroit; hit Eight Mile Road! And I don't give a damn if they are black or white, or if they wear Superfly suits or blue uniforms with silver badges. Hit the road."

Families of black friends tell me they felt abandoned, left, forgotten. They were told they were not worthy. People like local author and poet dream hampton write hauntingly about what it was like to be left behind, to be the ones still standing as everything collapsed around them. In her essay "Things I Lost in the Fire," published in the book *A Detroit Anthology*, she tells the story of losing her childhood home to arson:

"By the late eighties, the black families on our block who could always afford new model cars disappeared to exotic places like Southfield and Oak Park," she remembered. "Chandler Park, where I had several birthday parties and spent most weekends, became off-limits because of the shootouts. Still we stayed. . . . I'd long ago moved on from that neighborhood, but I did move back to Detroit a few years ago. I want to be a part of the rebuilding of my beloved city. But first, I must tear down the scorched brick house that was my home for most of my life."

How do you square that narrative? How do you salve wounds this deep? How do you not cry at the shitty irony of the fact that today almost nobody in Detroit can get a mortgage, black or white? The more things change, the more they stay the same. Real estate continues to be at the crux of this city's struggles as it looks to rebuild.

I wish I had answers, but I don't. I have to make peace with my own family history and my grandparents' white flight out of Denver for the safety of the suburbs. My mother tells me it wasn't because of race; it was because of forced busing—my grandfather didn't want her and my aunts traveling on the bus for hours each day when there was a neighborhood school just down the block. Were we part of the problem in Denver, even as my family, like so many white families here in metro Detroit, claim that race was not a factor? I am in no place to judge those who left and those who stayed except to look into my own heart and history and try to understand and empathize with the hard choices everyone had to make during an ugly—if not yet over—part of our country's history.

Like Detroit, Matilda had a glamorous past. She was the home of Arthur and Nona Herzog.

Nona Herzog was a great beauty with flaming red hair who grew up in London, studied at the Sorbonne, modeled Parisian couture, and immigrated to Detroit with her family after World War II. Arthur Herzog Jr. grew up a fashionable gent in New York City, a man of means sufficient to allow him to lead a life befriending and composing with all manner of musicians in Manhattan's late-night jazz clubs. He cowrote "God Bless the Child" with Billie Holiday and was friends with Nina Simone. But he left New York for Detroit during its boom years, attracted to the electricity and opportunity of the city.

"He was doing PR and worked for Paramount doing advance PR for new films," said Greg Herzog, who is the only surviving son of Arthur and his first wife, Leepee. "He once commented to me that Detroit would be an easier place to do it than New York."

Our new neighbors love to tell stories about the couple and show us memorabilia from the house. They regale us with stories of Arthur and Nona's frequent dinner parties and Sunday salons for neighbors, visiting musicians, and Hollywood types. When guests would arrive, Arthur, who had a penchant for white linen jumpsuits, would greet them at the door by taking cocktail orders. He would have the entire menu planned and typed up, course by course, on his electric script typewriter and then would preserve a copy and the guest list in a collection of books.

"That was a tradition that he kept up for most of his life," Gregory tells me.

I instantly decide to honor it, starting with the first dinner party I can throw in the house, whenever that may be.

Our neighbors Kathy and Mark Beltaire were friends with Arthur and Nona, and as they tell us more about Matilda's famous past life, neither Karl nor I can believe the serendipity. As a fellow musician, Karl is enamored by the idea that he will own the home that once housed a famous jazz lyricist. He can hear the sound of Arthur's piano rolling through the house and feels the inspiration of his presence. I feel the family's literary prowess, hoping it will rub off on me: Arthur's first son, Arthur Herzog III, was a journalist and a novelist who worked for *Harper's*, *Esquire*, and the *New York Times Magazine* and once spoke at a Metro Detroit Book and Author Society luncheon alongside Madeleine L'Engle. Arthur Jr.'s granddaughter, Amy, was a 2012 finalist for the Pulitzer Prize in drama for her play *4,000 Miles*. I can't believe all the connections that come with this house. Whenever I walk down the stairs, trailing my hand on the banister, I imagine all the times Nona did the same thing. It gives me great comfort.

When Arthur first arrived in Detroit, he had an office in the extravagant Fox Theatre building downtown, right near the movie action. Arthur never kept a car in the Motor City, choosing instead to walk the five blocks home to his apartment in the Seville Hotel, which was run by Herman Radner, father of comic Gilda Radner of *Saturday Night Live* fame. The Seville is where everyone who was anyone stayed, and Arthur was there in the center of it all. Greg remembers boyhood walks with his father from the Seville or the Fox to Wayne State University or to Hudson's, the famed department store that is long gone but still a part of Detroit lore. Old photographs show elegantly dressed men and women streaming out of its doors into a downtown bustling with office workers and residents, shops lining every side of Woodward Avenue. It was a glamorous time. The Detroit of dreams.

"He carved a pretty comfortable life for himself," said Greg, who teaches cosmochemistry at Rutgers University. "He knew all the clubs where the visiting jazz musicians would come, and he would go there and invite the musicians back to his place for a late dinner. Many were grateful for a place to go that wasn't a hotel or a restaurant."

Karl and I decide to retrace Arthur's path from work to the Seville and try to imagine his Detroit.

Today the Fox Theatre is the headquarters of Mike and Marian Ilitch's $5.5 billion empire, which encompasses Little Caesars Pizza and the Detroit Red Wings and Detroit Tigers. They bought the building in 1987, when it had been long shuttered. After Arthur's era, the Fox struggled—like Detroit itself—falling into disrepair, going from hosting Elvis Presley and Motown artists to scraping by on ticket sales from martial arts flicks in the 1970s, to finally closing for good. The Ilitches invested $12 million to refurbish the property —including the gold leafing—and reopened the theater as a performance hall, installing their offices on the upper floors.

When we get to the spot where the Seville is supposed to stand, however, we find no sign of the place that touched so many lives and that we are now connected to through Arthur and Nona. We learn that the building succumbed to the wrecking ball in 2002. And the path through the area, which is sandwiched between downtown and Midtown, is nothing but empty lots, razor wire, and the skeletons of buildings. Weeds sprout through fissures in the concrete, and party stores sling Colt 40s.

We spot Comet Bar, a shot-and-beer punk-rock joint, so we stop in for, well, a shot and a beer. Even though we have Maddie and Leroy with us, the Comet bartenders welcome us in. They have a grill running in the backyard, slapping out burgers, while patrons flaunt Michigan's smoking ban inside. We have to enjoy this spot while we can: the Comet is about to go the way of the Seville. The Ilitches are planning a new $450 million hockey arena for the Detroit Red Wings right in the path of Arthur's old life. New neighborhood districts are conceived, new housing, new retail—an attempt to bring the area back to the lively one Arthur once knew.

Arthur made Detroit his home until his death in 1983, staying even after the riots, when so many other people he knew fled. His only change was trading in his downtown world for the West Village, where he met Nona. "I don't think Dad ever even thought about leaving Detroit," Gregory says. "That's not a conversation we ever even had. He was perfectly happy and settled there. Detroit became his home."

Gregory remembers visiting the neighborhood and it being "rough around the edges," though he still keeps a memory of wooden swans in Nona's gardens.

"Are they still there?" he asks.

Sadly, they are not. But I can still see signs of her everywhere. She loved roses and peonies, and one rosebush remains, mostly mangled, climbing the remains of a quaint basket-weave fence that separates our yard from the West Village Association–owned lot next door. Kathy, too, remembers those gardens and the West Village being rough around the edges when she moved in and befriended Nona in the 1970s. Kathy grew up in Detroit and didn't want to leave the city, even as everyone told her to go. Instead, she found the West Village and was drawn to it by a sense of revival and resurgence she hoped would soften and refine those rough edges. Restaurants were opening, young people like her were moving in, and the neighborhood seemed to be reviving after some difficult years. So many people had left that the area was in danger of disappearing to the urban renewal wrecking ball. But Nona and Kathy were staying put. The two ladies, with a group of others, lobbied to have the area listed on the National Register of Historic Places. In 1980 they got their wish and preserved the area so people like Karl and I could come and make it their home too.

Jim Boyle and his wife, Mary Trybus, share a similar story about the appeal of the neighborhood when they came in the late 1990s. They felt the energy and the sense of community. And now here Karl and I are, fifteen years later, saying the same things. The neighborhood, we realize, has been at this tipping point before. It has risen and fallen many times. The area's strength isn't in its location, development potential, or in the restaurants we hope might open someday. No, like Detroit itself, the West Village's resilience lies with the people who call it home, who persist in believing despite the odds. Mark and Kathy Beltaire. Bob and Carol Rhodes. Vittoria Katanski and Bill Swanson. All of the neighbors who now surround us and welcome us home, home to Nona's Place, as everyone still calls this house.

"Nona was a very independent, sometimes opinionated, but very good, loyal friend and always great company," says Kathy. "She was a lover of good food and wine, beautiful gardens, dogs and cats. She had a great laugh. She was the whole package."

Nona finally did leave her beloved house in 2002. The way Kathy tells it, Nona grabbed a cab and went to the airport. She didn't even pack a bag. She bought a ticket at the airline counter and flew home to London with nobody in Detroit the wiser. She passed away seven years later, having never returned to Detroit. She sold the house soon after leaving, the demarcation line of Before Decline (BD) and After Decline (AD).

What era we are in now, I don't know. AAD? After After Decline? Regardless, our house is Nona's Place, the pride of a bold, audacious woman who spoke her mind. It doesn't bother me that all the neighbors still refer to it as that; it feels like an honor, one that connects me to both Detroit and to Colorado, where old homesteads and ranches are almost always known by the original owners' names long after they've gone.

◆ ◆ ◆

After the bankruptcy announcement, friends call, parents call, Facebook acquaintances inquire: *Are you sure? It's not too late to back out. Come home. Come back to New York. What about Austin, Philly, Denver . . . any city that isn't Detroit?* But we hold firm. With everything we are learning about the city, about Arthur and Nona and those who have come before us, we feel bullish about our future here.

And paradoxically the bankruptcy makes us feel cautiously optimistic, like maybe the city has hit bottom and can only rebound. We weren't counting on that when we decided to move to Detroit; we took the city as it was. But having not lived here through the dark times and arriving in the city as a middle-class couple of some means, we have the privilege of thinking that the city's bankruptcy, fingers crossed, might be good. Nobody is certain, though, what the results will be. National stories say it's a blessing. National stories say Detroit is dead. Who wants a bankrupt city? Who will be the winners, and who will be the losers in the final outcome? If the results are good, will they be widespread enough to impact those who never left or couldn't leave, those who are scraping by day to day, the idea of rehabbing a house in their home city not an option or even a viable dream? Or will they only be good for people like Karl and me?

After all, in downtown and Midtown, residential occupancy rates hover around 97 percent, rents are soaring, and the streetlights are on. The glorious skyscrapers of boomtown Detroit are being buffed up and reopened as firms of all shape and size look to return to the city, to what they see as their ancestral roots. Downtown is buzzing with health, education, and tech workers. Whole Foods has opened, the first national grocer in Detroit in a decade. Shinola, the luxury brand known for watches, leather goods, and bikes, chose to call Detroit home after a national search. Young families and singles are living the urban lifestyle familiar to any city: six-figure incomes, $4 lattes, dinners out, shows, artisanal anything.

But get outside the golden bubble—the 7.2 square miles that make up downtown and Midtown—and the story is different. Looking toward downtown from Gratiot Avenue, it actually does look like a golden bubble: you can see where the lights stop. This Detroit is where fire stations are stocked with donated toilet paper and the city's 39 percent poverty rate is tangible. The streets are lined with falling-down homes, and both people and feral dogs scrape to get by. The area near Gratiot and Seven Mile Road is one that breaks my heart every time Karl and I drive through on our way to dinner at Capers Steakhouse, a family-owned restaurant that has served steak by the ounce since 1982. The blight here is not your picturesque "ruin porn" of the train station and Packard Plant; the seven miles between downtown and Capers is just sheer abandonment on display. Whereas the neighborhood surrounding our new house is pockmarked with wreckage, this is full-on Chernobyl, with once-beautiful buildings spilling their guts through gaping holes where windows and front doors once stood. These properties aren't even boarded up; we can see straight into the heart of them, rubble everywhere and the shadowy shapes of a few humans who must be taking respite from the night under what's left of the roofs. And yet people and businesses like Capers continue to eke out existences on the borders of this urban moonscape.

It's easy to say that this is a tale of two cities, but that implies two equal halves. There are not. There are 7.2 square miles of means and access and education—and 132 without.

As soon as we signed our lives over to Matilda, Karl and I had to start considering our place in all of this. I can't know what this level of desperation is, what it means to be poor and black in Detroit, but I do have some inkling of how it feels to watch others succeed in a place you can no longer afford. So as I learn the history of my new home, I try to recognize the privilege that has allowed me to come here naively and with gleeful intentions of buying a cheap house without recognizing everything that has led to getting us here. Who had to lose for me to win?

We can't know what will happen with the bankruptcy, what

this will mean for Detroit and Detroiters. But I hope we can prove that, come what may, we want to stay. This is our hometown now, and if I am anything, I am loyal. I want to do right by the memory of Nona and Arthur and all of our neighbors and all of the other people who have believed, even as the rest of the world can only see a dead city.

CHAPTER SEVEN

THE HISTORY OF THE HOUSE weighs heavy on us as we start thinking about how to both honor the ghosts of Nona's Place and make it our own.

When we found Matilda, the only historical elements left were the ribbon-oak floors, which were marred and missing in places; a bit of the trim; the fireplace, which was black from char; the front door, which had met the wrong end of a hammer; and the octagonal tile floors in the bathrooms. But with just those clues we can sense that she is formal and traditional, definitely a grander dame than I ever imagined sharing my life with. So Karl and I are in a conundrum about respecting those good bones while also designing a home that reflects how we live. We have the clutter, chaos, fur, and drool that come with sixteen paws' worth of critter. We read books and magazines, and I like being surrounded by those old friends. We are not formal or minimalist people. I don't want a *Dwell*-worthy modern miracle—I just want a home.

Karl and I have been married a year and together for five, but we're just beginning to learn each other's tastes. We didn't decorate in Brooklyn so much as just combine our belongings into one apartment. Here, our aesthetic differences are definitely emerging. Karl is drawn to basic, primary colors, like fire-engine red and blueberry, while I go for rusts, silvery greens, and twilight blue. Karl trends toward midcentury modern, despite a habit of clutter, while I enjoy the warmth of a Craftsman bungalow mixed with certain Eames pieces. We each have very strong opinions about what we do and do not like, so we've created a rule that if both of us don't agree on an item, we keep looking. We are still sleeping on a mattress on the floor because we've never found a mutually satisfactory bed frame. He wants a modern platform, while I prefer an old iron bedstead. When we do find something that excites both of us, we invariably balk at the price. At least the dogs like the current situation: they just wander onto our king-sized floor nest, all 165 pounds of them.

Still, we never sit down and have a conversation or develop a plan for the future of Matilda. Design decisions seem like they are part of some distant, hazy future. The great someday—you know, when we can afford it. So we are expecting there may be some, um, dramatic tension with only "industrial cottage"—meaning lots of wood, brick, and steel—as our guiding principle. We hope to keep it cheap, simple, and clean. We have no design professional out sourcing objects d'art; instead, we have some vague notion that when the time comes, we will get kitchen cabinets and fixtures from IKEA and buy old doors at salvage. In a fit of enthusiasm we create a Pinterest board to organize our ideas, but it quickly languishes. We spend more time creating lists in Google Docs, outlining all the decisions to be made and tasks accomplished. The main notes: a shower that Karl, who is six foot two, can stand under without banging his head and task lighting in the kitchen so I can stop chopping in shadows.

As a starting point we are using the architectural plans that Fatima had drafted and gave to us as part of the sale. Her vision was to open up the warren of rooms that once composed the kitchen and create one long expanse running the length of the house. I love the idea of a combined dining room and kitchen because it's ideal for parties. Everyone always gathers in the kitchen, so why not make it the heart of our entertaining space? I see the friends we have yet to make all standing around a big butcher-block island, drinking wine, chopping vegetables, laughing, and gossiping together. I see myself drinking coffee and reading the Sunday *New York Times* at the island while Karl makes scrambled eggs.

Our first task, however, is to get the house habitable—water, heat, and WiFi—before our lease in Ann Arbor runs out in just three short months. (Go ahead, start laughing. We will be joining you shortly.) To make that happen, Karl and I must face the fact that we're going to need some help. We want to do the work ourselves—this is the land of DIY, after all. Our friends Tris and Jason try to convince us that we can do it all, right down to installing the electrical service. I'd like to think that were true, but I know better. Karl isn't what you'd call handy, and I'm only handy by New York standards, meaning I can wield a screw gun in a pinch. I'm the outcast in my family of can-doers. My mother believes there's nothing she can't do without a trip to the library, and my father, well, he's my father. I'm certain my parents wonder how I graduated from college with fewer life skills than they sent me in with. But having grown up in this family of doers, I'm not sure how to hire someone either. So we call Dad for advice.

Dad didn't do homeowner projects; he dug giant pits in the hard rock of Colorado to lay pipe for things like wastewater treatment plants. The few times he did work on projects like mine, they almost never went well. Homeowners are nightmare clients, he would say. They want everything right now and think they deserve a deal. They want you right this very instant when they have an emergency, but when the job is done, you are no longer good enough to breathe their air. His experience with homeowners was that no good deed goes unpunished. So Dad's advice was pretty simple: don't be an entitled asshole.

Contractors, he said, have a right to feed their families. Don't look for cheap; seek quality work at a fair price. That is so important that Dad had this bit of philosophy inscribed on the back of his Bear Excavating business cards: "The bitterness of poor quality and workmanship remains long after the sweetness of the low bid is forgotten." I remember reading that as a kid, and it's always stuck with me. Be direct and decisive, he added. Know your budget and be honest about it. Pay on time. Look for someone who is a partner, who asks good questions and seems to care about the answers. Look for someone who can make suggestions and offer alternatives. Go with your gut and understand that your contractor is worth every dime because that's the person who will make the project either a dream or a nightmare. You're going to be more married to them, he tells me, than to Karl. Finally, make sure they are bonded and insured.

Armed with that advice, Karl starts calling contractors to come and look at Matilda. It is a real test of our marriage for me to give up control and trust him. I'm the one who has done this before, after all. I'm the one who pays attention to minutia. I'm the ideal candidate for calling contractors. But Karl hasn't started working yet, while I've had to leave the lazy days of my fellowship behind for my new position at *Crain's Detroit Business*. I simply don't have time to be in charge. I hold my breath and hope that we can get through it without another granola-bar-throwing incident. Or divorce.

When only two contractors agree to meet with us, I first blame Karl and assume he must be doing something wrong. But it's not Karl's fault: everyone is either too busy or doesn't want to work in Detroit. Mostly they don't want to work in Detroit. That should have been our first sign that Matilda was destined to be a high-maintenance relationship.

The first contractor seems nice enough, but he begins criticizing everything about the house almost immediately. It's too big of a project, not worth the investment. He scoffs at our budget. Worse, he is incredulous that we are willing to invest any money in Detroit. We explain that this is a great town and a lot of people are interested in living here. We tell him about our neighbors, who have been so warm and welcoming.

"Are your neighbors lying to you?" he asks. "You know your rims are going to get jacked or the entire car stolen, most likely. So just be prepared."

He never even calls us back with a bid.

When Calvin Garfield walks into the Tim Horton's near the house, I'm not sure what to think. He is an elegant man wearing a Brooks Brothers–esque button-down, slacks, and loafers. I don't see any calluses on his hands or grease under his nails. He looks nothing like the roughnecks I know, who, even when they clean up for a business meeting, can't hide the dark black stains under their fingernails. But I give him the benefit of the doubt, knowing he already knows more about the project than me because he worked with Alyson and Fatima as they tried to keep their dream alive.

Calvin starts out by asking all the right questions. He wants to know how we want to use the space, wants to understand our priorities so we can focus the budget in those areas. He wants to know how we envision our life in the house. He even makes suggestions on how to adapt the plans to save money. We tell him we are still figuring out how to fund the project, so it probably needs to happen in phases. He says he is comfortable with that and thinks he can get us into the house by early August—in an urban-camping kind of way. When he tells us that he lives in Detroit, grew up in Detroit, raised his kids in Detroit, and was a city building inspector for much of his career, we're all but sold on him.

Cal agrees to go over the plans and send us an updated, phased bid by the weekend.

In the meantime I get a text from my father with a bit more advice.

"A couple of ideas to get you started: sell raffle tickets to see who comes closest to naming the exact number of the renovation cost. Also, invest in a barbecue to cook on and a chamber pot and a large volume of candles."

"That's not funny," I respond.

"It's more than I had sometimes when I was trailing sheep through the hills."

When I open Calvin's spreadsheet, I try not to hyperventilate.

We may need that barbeque and chamber pot.

We haven't even started the project, and we're already over budget if we want anything close to a finished home. The full budget, which includes everything except rebuilding the garage and porch, tops $300,000. Thankfully Calvin broke it into phases, the first of which meets our initial $100,000 budget and gets us moved in at the end of August—but with no drywall, no finished floors, no doors. It really will be urban camping. Even worse, we have to choose between having windows or having plumbing. Matilda has forty-six windows, most of which are busted up or missing, and they need replacing. But the price of doing that with Detroit Historic District Commission–sanctioned models—nearly $30,000—is nearly the same as what it will cost to plumb the entire house and install the furnace. We can afford only one: windows or water.

I don't even know what to say when I come downstairs to show Karl. We both just sit there dumbfounded. But this is the reality of rehabbing these old houses: the cost of acquisition isn't the problem; it's always the cost of improvements.

We could try to find another contractor, but we've already fallen in love with Cal—we're already on a nickname basis—and believe he is the right one to do the work. We love that he is from Detroit, never left, even when his family did, and raised his kids in the city. We love that his son, Christian, and daughter, Whitney, work with him. Our preliminary meetings always run long because Cal is a talker and we end up in long conversations about books—he's a C. S. Lewis fanatic—jazz, and his love of the city. He tells us stories about his childhood in Korea, where his father was a missionary, and about his church and the old pipe organ he spent years restoring for them.

Christian, however, is the strong, silent type. He doesn't wax philosophic like his dad; he often lovingly rolls his eyes at Cal. But he, too, is fully engaged with the world and living in it on his terms. He lived in Boston and worked in finance after college, but he grew to hate that life. So he called home one afternoon and told Cal he couldn't do it anymore. He hopped a flight back to Detroit, and the two went into business together. Now the father-son duo is rehabbing Detroit, one home at a time.

I think about my dad's business card and know that Cal and Christian are our guys. We'll find a way to make it work even though the numbers are daunting and we don't know how to choose between windows or water.

When I e-mail Cal to tell him we want to move forward, his return e-mail tells me we've made the right choice:

> I hope this is but the beginning of a great chapter in your lives, one you will look back on with fond and deeply satisfying memories. Churchill observed that we build our houses (I think he actually said "buildings") and then find that our houses shape us. Three houses have functioned that way for me: the one I grew up in Korea, the one my family lives in now, and the one we spent more than ten summers at on Cape Cod. Many of the best memories of my life are inseparably tied to those places. Let's make Van Dyke Place that for you.

Construction on Matilda starts during a blistering hot streak in July, when the temperatures are an unusual 100 degrees and the humidity nearly 100 percent. Cal, Christian, and the demolition crew are working inside the house, which is stifling because it's still boarded up. The air is thick with plaster dust that, when combined with sweat and humidity, leaves white streaks of salt residue on the men's faces. But we have a rapidly approaching deadline, and there is a lot to be done.

I can't even imagine how miserable they must be. I remember Dad sweltering in the un–air conditioned cab of a tractor during the dog days of August. He always told me he preferred to work in the bitter cold because at least he could put on another layer; in the heat you can only strip down so far. I tell this to Cal and Christian, and they are divided in opinion. Cal will take the heat; Christian prefers the cold. I'm impressed that instead of collapsing in air conditioning at night, Christian plays in a recreational soccer league, often enduring double-headers against the city's Chaldean and Latino teams.

I stop by each evening before driving back to Ann Arbor, bringing ice waters, Gatorade, and sometimes beers. We stand outside and chat, them taking a break to fill me in on the day's progress. It is amazing to watch how fast the house changes. On Monday it looks like a decaying tomb. On Tuesday rubble cascades down the stairs and pours through the open walls, and lathe and nails stick out everywhere like a game of Jenga. By Friday the house is empty. The interior walls are completely stripped down to the studs, the floors are swept, and I can see straight through the house from the front yard to the backyard. I am so glad we hired a team to knock out the demo in a week instead of the months it would have taken us. This is a luxury, I know. The other couples we are meeting are taking the long, room-by-room road. But most of them aren't starting with empty shells; they can at least turn on lights or run water.

"What color do you want your windows to be?" Cal asks one evening as we stand outside together. His voice fades under the loud, persistent hum of the generator that runs from sunup to sundown, six days a week. Every day, Monday through Saturday, they fire up that generator at first light and don't cut it until after dark some days. Initially I assume it must drive all of our neighbors to the edge of insanity, that hum that shakes your brain, but they tell me not to worry, the sound of progress outweighs the inconvenience. Still, I know I've heard cheers when Van Dyke Place suddenly goes silent at 10 p.m.

We have to choose our window color because, after much deliberation, Karl and I decided to go with windows, not water. It sounds crazy, I know. How are we going to move into a house without water or heat? But we want to get the house structurally sound and secure before we worry about what's inside the walls.

"What color do you want the windows to be?" he asks again.

I stare at Cal blankly, fully unprepared for this question.

"Window colored?" I suggest.

At no point in the debate over windows or water had I thought about the color of our windows. I didn't even know windows had colors. But Matilda's windows are historically appropriate six-over-ones, Cal tells me, made of wood and featuring six-panel detailing and true muntins on the upper panes. The exterior is clad in aluminum and can be any color approved by the Historic District Commission, which in the case of Georgian Revivals is limited to certain whites, grays, greens, blacks, yellows and browns, and a few blues. Suddenly having to decide how to spend nearly $30,000 is paralyzing. What if I get the color wrong? Growing up, even picking out a $5.99 pack of women's bikini-cut underwear could be enough to paralyze my mother. There was no money to do it over, to change her mind if she made the wrong choice. I remember her and I both staring at the wall of options, overwhelmed. And now I'm contemplating sums that seem unfathomable.

"White?" I suggest, pausing for validation. "That's what they were before, right?" I trail on. "We know white is okay with the commission. Plus, I think black would make the house look like she has black eyes."

Cal agrees.

One decision down, uppity-bazillion more to go.

We've only been at this a few weeks, and I already feel like I'm playing a never-ending speed round of whack-a-mole. There is always another long list of decisions awaiting us when I visit. Sometimes they are big choices, other times minutia, but there is a mind-numbing volume of them. It never dawned on us, for example, that we'd need to know *right now*, while the walls are still being demoed, what type of light fixtures we planned to install. We figured we'd pick those out when we actually had electricity and could ditch the industrial construction lights powered by generators that are strung up everywhere like an extreme-DIY-chic take on holiday twinkle lights. But no, Cal needs to know now so he can tell the electrician where to install hundreds of boxes.

Do we want a chandelier in the dining room?

Will it be on a dimmer switch?

Will there be ceiling fans? With or without lights?

Canned lights or actual fixtures? Where would you like the canned lights placed?

The drawings show canned lights here, here, and here, but is that where you want them?

Will the bathroom sconces go above the medicine cabinets or along the sides?

Will there be two or three pendant lights over the island?

How long is the island, so we know how to center them?

Will you want task lighting?

Yes! Yes! That one I can answer. *I do want task lighting in the kitchen.*

Mostly, though, I just stare at them. I'm convinced Cal and Christian think I am mentally slow because the only expression I can regularly muster is that of a deer in headlights. I've made so many decisions that I feel like I only have bad ones left in me.

But already I know, despite the finances, that hiring Cal and Christian was one of our best ones. We're already hearing from others about how much they hate and don't trust their contractors. But that's not the case for us. In just a few weeks they've already become more like our friends than just our contractors. I've told Cal about Dad and growing up out West. He tells me about his church and his life filled with adventures and travels. Long afternoon chats often start with statements such as, "When I was living in Paris studying languages . . . " He tells me about his years as a city building inspector, when he often saw the worst parts of humanity laid bare. But we also like to share funny animal videos we find on the Internet. We both love the one with a dog dressed as a spider terrorizing strangers. We can't stop laughing. And we love to talk about books and movies. When I ask whether he watches *Breaking Bad*, which Karl and I have just started, I'm curious about his reaction. I assume the show will be too dark and violent for his tastes.

"I've never liked Greek tragedies, but *Breaking Bad* is so excellent because it's like a Greek tragedy without being moralistic or didactic," he says.

You just never know where Cal is going to take you.

As I get to know him and Christian, I begin relying on them not just for their technical skills but also their opinion and guidance about what needs to be done, what can be done, and what should be done aesthetically. Cal has worked jobs where the cheapest path of least resistance is the one the client wants; he's also worked high-end projects. One client had him clad her house in hand-cut Italian stone—twice—because she didn't like the first color she had chosen. We're somewhere in the middle. This is a once-in-a-lifetime event; this is our dream home. There are no do-overs. So although we are budget conscious, we are also attentive to doing things right the first time rather than settling for a cheap temporary solution. We're not looking for high-end luxury finishes—no Italian stone for us—but we do want Matilda to reflect the level of love and care we are taking to bring her back to life. We want her to stand for another hundred years.

When Cal tells us we must have a powder room on the first floor, however, we balk. This seems like an obvious spot to cut corners, as Matilda never had one. Sure, a bathroom on the first floor would be nice, but it's not a necessity. He and Christian, however, are adamant that this is a bad choice. First, they say, a powder room would improve our resale price if we were ever to sell. Jim Boyle, who is sitting in on this conversation, concurs. You can't have too many bathrooms, says the man with three children and only one full bath and a powder room. Second, Cal says, it will be easier for parties. He has beautiful ideas about how a house should work and flow, and he doesn't want people traipsing through our "private space," as he calls it, upstairs.

And, he says, he has an idea . . .

Like Stacy always has a theory, Cal always has an idea.

Christian shoots me a look, the mock-pleading one we have developed that says, *See what I have to put up with?* Over the weeks a comfortable banter has befallen the house with all of us gently teasing each other. Sometimes they all gang up on me; sometimes Christian is the object of our harassment. But most frequently it's me and Christian making jokes at his dad's expense. I feel like I'm back home with my dad and Matt, with Christian playing Matt's role.

Cal would like to take the existing closet on the main floor and turn it into built-in bookshelves for me. Then, he says, we can just cheat a few feet out of the living room and build both a hall closet right by the front door and a powder room. It's a vision that is hard to resist, although I don't know how we can save the existing "closet," which to my eye looks more like a moldering wooden box hanging off the house like a broken arm. Plus, I am still fretting about how to pay for the plumbing that would go into this mythical bathroom.

"Maybe in the next phase," I suggest.

Cal and Christian contemplate my answer and then, in the nicest way possible, refuse to accept it. They tell us it will cost next to nothing to frame the powder room and new closet now because the walls are already open; it will cost more, they say, to do it later. So they propose a compromise: if we buy the fixtures when it's time, they will cover the costs of framing and drywalling those rooms. Cal is that adamant about us having a bathroom—and about getting to build in the bookshelves, which he already has an idea on how to design . . .

I look around to find Karl and see what he thinks, but he has disappeared. He often wanders off during these discussions because the nuance and details overwhelm him. Still, he wishes he could be onsite more often and part of the daily dialogue. He's stuck in Ann Arbor packing us for the looming move while I go to work every day at *Crain's*. I know he is languishing there, so desperate to get to Detroit and begin our new life. I know it's hard for him to watch as I grow more familiar with Detroit and make most of the decisions about our house on my own. I try to include him, but like today's bathroom discussion, everything happens so fast and so furious that there often isn't time. To combat that isolation and disconnection, he's started bringing Cal, Christian, and the crew a late lunch of pizza and beer on Friday afternoons. This reminds me of my mother, who was known to show up on Dad's job sites with chili and cornbread or stew and rolls. I try to join them when I can, and we all sit on the floor in what will someday be the living room, eating off a makeshift table of plywood and drywall buckets.

Afterward Karl typically wanders outside to weed the front walk, a path of uneven brick pavers that gives the house the air of "overgrown estate." This is where he has disappeared to during the bathroom discussion. I stand and watch him for a moment, touched by his actions. This is his way of contributing to Matilda, of building toward our future, the only way he knows how.

"This is one of the few things I can do," he says. "I can't do carpentry or plumbing or whatever, but I can weed."

The weeds may overtake the rest of the lawn while the front door remains nailed shut and our porch light dangles by its wires, but not a weed can be found between those pavers for the rest of the summer.

CHAPTER EIGHT

I ENTER THE CODE to the contractors' lockbox on the side door, care-fully extract the key, and let myself in. The front door is still sealed like a tomb, so everyone comes and goes through the side door. It's dark and still inside the house. A shaft of fading sun streams through a window and illuminates the pink staircase from above. I like to come here late in the day, after the crews are gone, to sit and think and enjoy some alone time in the house. The stairs offer the best van-tage point for looking out over all of the work that is done—and even more that is still yet to be accomplished.

I find myself talking to Matilda as if she were an old friend, discussing my hopes and dreams for our life. I tell her about Karl. I ask her what she wants, what we should do, and how we're going to figure out how to get the money to bring her back to life. I walk through each room, touching the bare studs, using my toe to trace outlines in the dust of where we will install cabinets and build walls. I get to know every quirk and oddity; I learn which floorboards squeak when I cross them and which stair treads to skip. I measure distances and try to imagine what she will look like, understand her personality.

As I sit on the stairs, I know I have to face facts: we are running out of money and out of time. The realities of what seemed like a funny lark just a few months ago—urban camping with a grand piano and sixteen paws' worth of critter—are sinking in. In just a few short weeks we are scheduled to move in and will be living without water or power, unable to charge our phones, cook, or even shower. We'll be dependent upon the neighbors' kind offers of bathrooms and laundry. We won't even have walls.

What should we do? I ask Matilda over and over. *What should we do?*

We knew early on that there wasn't enough money, and that the $100,000 we did have would quickly disappear into the walls. But I thought I'd be able to find a construction loan by now, some way to pay for the plumbing and heating and drywall and insulation and everything else that we know the house needs to be habitable. But I haven't found the money to pay for the things we expected, let alone all the things nobody could. Like a $9,000 bill for dentils.

Don't know what dentils are? Neither did we. Look up at the roofline of any historic building and you'll probably see them. They are on the Parthenon. They are on the White House. And they are most certainly on Matilda. You are looking for the small blocks attached under the eaves that sort of look like teeth. That which makes sense because the word *dentil* gets it origin from the Latin *dens* for tooth. But unlike teeth, dentils don't do anything. They don't protect anything. They are purely decorative. And Matilda has almost a hundred of them, all of which are rotting and need to be replaced.

I'd like to skip this repair and do it "someday" in the future. But the dentils are just one part of a larger problem: the eaves—where the roof overhangs and forces water away from the walls. The fascia and soffit that make up the underside of the eaves are rotting away and are hanging on by just a few nails. A good rain or heavy Michigan snowstorm could start to pull them all down. Unfortunately the eaves are not a "repair later" situation. And if we're going to rebuild all of the eaves back to original condition, it makes no sense to put back cracked, moldy dentils. Nope, they are a package deal.

Cal discovered the problem as framing crews were rebuilding the crumbling south wall of the house. As he poked into the eaves, inspecting how to tie the new brick wall into the old roof, Christian got quite the surprise. Dirt, squirrel carcasses, and rodent nests rained down on his head, covering him in debris. He stood there for a moment stunned. Cal and I couldn't help but laugh at the absurdity of what had just happened—until the scent caught us all. It smelled worse than death. Not even the old Stinkmobile was this bad. The only time I've ever smelled something even as remotely disgusting was on the eve of Stacy's thirtieth birthday. We had driven up to her family's lake cabin for the weekend, but when we arrived near midnight, tired and hungry, we discovered we didn't have the right key. While we stood in the sallow moonlight, fiddling with the lock, trying every key on Stacy's ring, Maddie took off into the woods. A revolting stench announced her return. The only thing that could make a dog smell that bad, Stacy determined, was if she rolled in a "turducken of death"—death cooked inside death cooked inside death cooked inside death.

Gagging, we loaded Maddie into the back of the Saab and then hung our heads out the windows as we drove the dark back roads in search of somewhere to stay for the night. Looking in the rearview mirror, I could see Maddie grinning with sheer joy. Most motels we encountered were full for the night, so when we saw the vacancy sign advertising rooms for $30 a night, Stacy and I looked at each other and shrugged. We got a key and then hustled Maddie inside and straight to the tub where Stacy helped me wash dirt, blood, and feces off of my dog. We dried her off, cleaned up the bathroom, and finally headed for the one small bed. As we settled into the threadbare blankets, Maddie jumped up and burrowed between us. Stacy awoke on her birthday to find my dog's butt on her pillow, smelling faintly of death and cheap shampoo.

I smile, remembering that trip and thinking that if Stacy and I weren't already bonded for life, that experience made it so. She says she's loyal because my life gives her great fodder for cocktail parties, but we both know it's because she's the sister I never had and I'm the one she got to choose. I know she will laugh when I call and explain that we now know why Matilda smelled old and musty. And she will be there to empathize when I tell her the bad news: we need to replace the roof, rebuild the eave soffits, and have new dentils cut out of cedar and installed. A complete new hat for Matilda.

In total it will be a $27,000 bill. A $27,000 bill that I have no idea how to pay. I know it makes more sense in the long run, both financially and structurally, to do it all at once, but it's a hard expense to swallow. We could do everything but the dentils, but we are in a historic neighborhood. If you start with dentils, you finish with dentils or face the possible fines and wrath of the Historic District Commission. These old homes take a lot of love and care; they aren't for those who want to do it on the cheap, I'm discovering.

"Matilda is one greedy bitch," Stacy says when I call and tell her.

In *Under the Tuscan Sun*, Frances Mayes makes it look so easy. She never seems to sweat the finances or the details. Even the setbacks are charming or zany: her husband tends grape vines, mows terraces, or sips espresso; my husband weeds the front walk. Her contractors laugh after pulling a giant boulder from the wall and causing the house to quake. Mine have nailed the petrified carcass of a squirrel to the wall through its eye socket. Christian's revenge, perhaps? But this is not Tuscany, it is Detroit, and somehow that creature will become our mascot. I had imagined Matilda as Bramasole—but with more grit, less money, and Michigan wine—when I should have been watching *The Money Pit*.

So far every bank we've approached has turned us down for financing. To get this far in the project, I busted open our 401(k)s, our break-glass-in-case-of-emergency option. I had hoped banks would look more favorably at us if we came to the table with $100,000 in cash. My plan was to use that capital to get some sort of construction loan and then put the money back into our retirement savings before the IRS started imposing penalties for early withdrawals. But that's not going to happen. The banks don't like my foreclosure or the fact that Karl hasn't started his new job yet, making us ineligible for even FHA's rehab program. But the bigger problem is that Matilda was just too cheap—she has no value to borrow against. If she's that cheap, the banks reason, she must not be worth enough to pour more money into. Plus, they are stymied by Matilda's lack of windows. They don't want to lend on anything that isn't habitable, which is what the boarded-up windows suggest. But we can't get rid of the boards and move in until we get a loan to pay for new windows. It's a chicken-and-egg conundrum.

This is Detroit, I plead. *Everything is cheap. Most of the city is boarded up. How are we supposed to rehab these houses if we can't get the money? How are houses supposed to be worth anything if nobody can rehab them?*

We get no sympathy. And it's not just us. All across the city we are meeting other couples running into similar problems. Banks just aren't equipped to handle projects like Matilda because the economics of Detroit make no rational sense. The houses are so far degraded that it often costs more to rehab them than they will be worth when finished. Take Matilda, for example: we know we will have to invest more than $300,000 to make her habitable again, but will be lucky to get a $150,000 appraisal—and then only if we bring dancing monkeys. Matilda would appraise for a cool half million in Denver and more than a million in Red Hook, which makes her a smart investment. But in Detroit the banks laugh us all the way to the, well, bank. The only sliver of hope comes from Talmer Bank and Trust, a local lender that suggests we come back when the house is finished. Then, depending on the appraisal and number of dancing monkeys, they might be able to write us a loan for the value of the house, a so-called cash-out refinance mortgage, so we can pay back any debts we accrue during construction. That means we have to come up with all the cash up front. It's not much, but it's the best option we've got.

This, however, is not a replicable, sustainable, or scalable way of rebuilding the city. Most people would have given up when the banks said no in the first place. How many people are willing to tap their 401(k)s and risk their retirement and entire financial future on a house in Detroit? Had we known how financially challenging this would be when we started, we might have walked away. Yes, I have a foreclosure on my credit report, which complicates things, but credit blemishes don't make me any different from most Detroiters—or many Americans. This city has no hope of recovering if middle-class couples like us, with $100,000 in cold hard cash, can't get a mortgage or a loan to buy and rehab properties. For the city to really revive, we must fix either the financing structure or the valuations. If we don't address this systemic problem, the city will continue to sit and rot, despite the voracious demand from people who want to call Detroit home.

◆ ◆ ◆

I grow more and more frustrated about our finances and the fact that I cannot find a way to raise the $60,000 we are already over budget— if we want windows and water plus a roof and eaves and dentils. But fretting about it isn't helping; instead, Karl decides we need a break. He books tickets on the Detroit Drunken Historical Society's kayak tour of the city's hidden canals. It seems like an excellent idea when he first proposes it. But standing here in a cove tucked away from the Detroit River, my heart racing with fear as I try to get into my boat, I want to murder him. I've never been in a kayak, and I have no idea how to paddle.

Karl spent his summers canoeing and kayaking across lakes in Tennessee, so he is completely calm and collected. He tells me it will all be fine, not to worry. I do not believe him. I'm absolutely phobic of water, convinced either I'm going to drown or, worse, fish might touch me. My fears are not unfounded: I did nearly drown in the Fruita pool as a kid. But that isn't even my real hang-up. It's my terror of fish, which I blame on my cousins. As kids, we went swimming in South Lake Tahoe, and they told me to be careful because the fish might bite me. Suddenly the image of fish silently gliding below me, just lurking as I bobbed like bait, was seared into my mind. Over the years these two incidents have blossomed into an irrational fear of water. I even keep a towel with me in the shower so that my face doesn't get wet. When Karl is feeling mischievous, he likes to steal it.

The last time I agreed to do something like this, Karl convinced me to canoe out to an island campsite in upstate New York. We arrived just as the sun was setting, forcing us to row out in the impending darkness. I was not a fan. As Karl propelled our boat across the water, I helplessly tried to paddle, convinced we would capsize at any moment. Leroy kept shifting his weight to get a better view, making the canoe dip and bob, while Maddie tried to jump in the lake. I never mastered paddling, but I got very good at reaching behind my back with the oar and smacking the dogs.

We survived, but I'm not certain how.

Today I take a deep breath, grit my teeth, and walk into the murky water. With a bit of awkwardness, I manage to get into the kayak and launch it into the park's quiet cove. I enjoy a mini-celebration in my mind until I realize the waves are pulling me away from shore and I don't know how to stop or turn. My first response is to close my eyes and hyperventilate. Thankfully a tour volunteer glides up next to me and offers a brief tutorial on how to paddle.

I've only mastered backward and going in circles when I realize everyone else is heading out of the cove and into rougher waters, a flotilla of brightly colored boats bobbing into the Detroit River. I can barely navigate the shallows and out of the cove; I am not emotionally or technically prepared for what lies ahead.

As we hit the rough water, my kayak decides to make a break for it and beeline toward the shipping lane. My brain can't connect the turn-right-by-paddling-left part of the program; I can't stop the pull of the current. I don't know what to do; I freeze up in terror. I am sobbing as another volunteer approaches me. He tells me it's going to be okay and tethers my kayak to his, paddling us toward the tranquil canal everyone else is entering.

Once we enter the calm waters, I am transported. It's like Venice in Detroit. These canals flow through the city's far east side, and there are houses and apartments abutting the banks. Some of the structures are luxury residences, whereas others are more working-class homes, but they all have their own boat docks and garages. Residents wave as we float by.

I rest my oar across the bow, letting myself drift through the leafy branches of the weeping willows that line the banks. It's hard to believe this is Detroit. You would never see it from the street. But that is the truth of Detroit: it isn't a showy, ostentatious city; it is a city of quiet splendor tucked around corners and secreted in canals. Pockets of beauty are everywhere—you just have to open yourself to them.

As I sit here soaking in Detroit, I realize I've been overlooking a solution to our money pit problem: my father. Thanks to the sale of Bear, Dad is liquid for the first time. In fact, he offered us a loan when Karl and I first started discussing Matilda, but I said no, assuming we'd be able to get a mortgage or construction loan. I also didn't want to take him up on his largesse, given that he didn't have much and know when he'd get work next. I've never asked him for money before, not even during the worst of times with Sean, when I was working multiple jobs and going to school full time. I always knew my family had no money to spare; every dime went into surviving and building the business. It was a huge sacrifice when he and Mom gave me $200 per month to help cover my living expenses while I was in college.

I can still hardly fathom asking for a loan from the man who just lost everything, but I'm desperate. When I ask, I'm wracked with guilt, but he waves off my worries.

"Something good had to come of this, kid," he says.

Still, it feels like blood money when the $75,000 check hits my bank account. I know where this money comes from, what it took to earn it, what it took to have access to it. I know the sacrifice he is making for me.

When Karl's dad and my grandparents and aunts also agree to help with both loans and gifts, we're overwhelmed by the support. We didn't expect them to understand—it is Detroit, after all. But they all want to be a part of this, of our future.

"Are things getting better there, Amy?" Grandma asks me when I talk to her on the phone. "What I hear on the news, it sounds like it might be. You be safe, honey."

I call Cal and Christian and tell them we have the money to keep moving forward. We can get water and windows, insulation and drywall. We can have the ribbon-oak floors repaired and refinished. We'll get our roof and dentils. There will be plenty of work left to do—painting, trim, tile, decorative items—but we can figure out how to pay for that later. Thanks to our families, we can actually rebuild this house strong enough to last another hundred years.

◆ ◆ ◆

Detroit, too, is struggling with its own impossible choices and seeking its own Hail Mary solutions. Banks, creditors, bond holders, everyone under the sun is claiming a piece of the decaying body known as the City of Detroit—that's the government, not the people—but there just isn't enough to go around. The city lacks the assets to both settle its debts and provide services to residents. Somebody is going to lose. But will it be the residents? Will their city services continue to dwindle? Will it be the retirees who gave their lives to this city? Will their pensions be slashed, their health care gutted, even as they are at their most vulnerable, unable to rebuild their savings or get new jobs? Or will it be the creditors? The latter wants the Detroit Institute of Arts's collection to be sold off—the city's jewel decimated—and profits split up among themselves: fire sale on a Picasso, bargain on the Renoir. Losing the art, one of the things that actually draws tourists—and their dollars—to this city would be a disaster. It would be like selling your car in a personal bankruptcy and then losing your job because you can't get to work. You don't get rid of the thing that allows you to earn. But the money has to come from somewhere. And it will either come by selling the art or cutting pensions.

Windows or water. Art or pensions. Detroit is a city of impossible choices.

There seem to be no good options for moving forward. Everything is murky. US bankruptcy judge Steven Rhodes, in whose courtroom this landmark bankruptcy case fell, clearly stated from the bench that this crisis has human costs and that the city cannot, must not, offer up the pensioners as collateral damage. But he also ruled that the pensions are contracts that can be severed in federal bankruptcy court, despite being protected by the Michigan constitution. It is a mixed message for the approximately twenty thousand pensioners whose financial futures hang in the balance.

From my position at *Crain's* I watch as Emergency Manager Kevyn Orr looks around for someone to call on for help because he just can't cut any deeper. Over the years the city had already slashed staff, stopped mowing parks, and decimated maintenance budgets. There is just no more to give.

The city's Hail Mary, like mine, comes from someone who has always been around, always been a supporter: Gerald Rosen. As the chief judge of the US District Court for the Eastern District of Michigan, Rosen has spent his career here either litigating or presiding over high-profile cases. When Detroit filed for bankruptcy protection, the judge tapped Rosen to act as his chief negotiator. Rosen quickly proves his reputation for hard bargaining by brokering a deal between the state, charitable foundations, corporations, and city that would raise $816 million over twenty years to save the DIA's art and prevent draconian cuts to pensions. If approved, the so-called Grand Bargain nest egg would support retirees, ensuring that fire and safety retirees—those who put their lives on the line daily—take no cut to their pension checks, while the general services retirees would face a 4.5 percent haircut and zero cost of living increases. Both, however, would face painful changes to their health care plans. In exchange the DIA's art collection would be spun off into a nonprofit trust, effectively removing it as an asset of the city forevermore. Never again could creditors try to hawk the city's *Thinker* sculpture by Rodin, the great murals of industry by Diego Rivera, or its piece of the great gate of Babylon, the *Gate of Ishtar*. The Rodins and Picassos would be safe. And pensioners could eat.

"This is not a bailout," says Michigan governor Rick Snyder as he lobbies the legislature to kick in the $195 million required of it by the plan. "This was truly an opportunity to come together and say, 'Let's change the direction of Detroit.' The city is already coming back in many ways, but from a public sector perspective, this really helps create an environment for success."

Both chambers of the state legislature signs off on the deal, confounding critics who had written off the city. And there were a lot of them. Detroit is the city everyone can agree to hate and judge from afar. It is a place other mayors can look down on and feel better than for never having fallen so low. The smugness is infuriating, whether it's coming from the Detroit suburbs or Atlantic City, whose mayor once boasted: "At least we're not Detroit." Detroit has become a symbol, representing more than just itself, but any ill anyone wants to ascribe to it, whether true or false.

But the legislature rejects that image of Detroit and instead agrees to pony up money from the state's tobacco settlement revenue in exchange for being shielded from future lawsuits related to the bankruptcy. Together, despite intrastate differences between conservative rural areas and the liberal cities, everyone comes together to try to rebuild this city stronger.

But the pensioners themselves have the final say. They must approve the deal—and even betting types are quiet on whether it will happen. And even if they reject the Grand Bargain, Judge Rhodes could still do a cram-down and approve the deal anyway. There is so much yet unknown in the bankruptcy. Kevyn Orr must first present his final plan of adjustment—his roadmap for how the city will accommodate its ravenous creditors and invest in city services and infrastructure—and get Rhodes to approve the plan as "feasible." It is a simple word but a high hurdle to cross.

◆ ◆ ◆

Matilda is eerily quiet after dark. As I prepare to leave after one of our evening chats, every noise seems amplified, startling. I never stay long when I'm here by myself, an hour tops, because after that the monsters in my mind start to come out.

What is that?

Is someone out there?

I darken my iPhone flashlight so nobody can tell I'm in the house.

Silently I creep down the stairs into the basement, where I think I might be able to get a view of their shadows through the glass-block windows.

There it is again. Voices.

I'm certain people out there are casing the joint. Even though Cal and Christian discussed posting a sign reading, "Plumbed in PEX not copper, please don't scrap" to deter potential thieves, we've never done it. And there is a vast wealth of tools inside the house that would bring in serious cash at the pawnshop. I've heard the horror stories of houses being repeatedly broken into as they were being reconstructed.

Maybe it's coming from the backyard? Are they looking around the house?

We have had two bathtubs stolen off the porch, but that turned out to be more help than hindrance. Both tubs were chipped during installation and Cal's perfectionist streak wouldn't let the minuscule damage stand. So he had them hauled to the back porch, which appeared to be one strong windstorm away from falling like matchsticks, while we all figured out a better home for them. Thieves solved the problem. But it was creepy to know that someone had been watching the house closely enough to know of the tubs' existence and when we would and would not be onsite.

I call Stacy in New York for help, deciding that calling the Detroit police is likely an exercise in futility. I know the statistics—the response time for death and maiming can be upward of an hour; I can't imagine what they'd be for "I hear noises."

Stacy keeps me on the phone, laughing at the ridiculousness of the situation, until I feel confident enough to creep back upstairs. I want to call Karl, but he's all the way in Ann Arbor—nothing he can do.

I open the side door—the only one that isn't boarded shut—and look out. Nothing. Then I hear the wind rustling and realize I just don't yet know Matilda's sighs and groans, how she reacts to wind and rain and snow. I was scared of my own house.

I lock the door, put the key in the lockbox, and start walking across the grassy lot next to the house toward my car. I was pleased to have a functioning streetlight when we first saw Matilda, but now that we own her and I'm coming and going at night, I'm deeply grateful for it. What was once an academic or intellectual appreciation is now an emotional connection. Before, the idea of an unlit city, of one where only half of the streetlights work, was an abstraction. I understood that it wasn't good, but I couldn't comprehend what it meant to actually live like that. I hadn't yet had the personal experience of driving for blocks and blocks and blocks, mile-long stretches, without any illumination. Businesses dark. Streets dark. Everything dark.

I used to grip my steering wheel a little tighter, on alert, jumping at shapes and sounds that seemed to move all around me as I drove back and forth between my office and the house, but after a few weeks I find that I no longer even notice the darkness unless I will myself to see. Detroit is already teaching me that we can acclimate ourselves to anything, to call anything normal. It's easy to stop seeing a problem.

But there are deep problems here that people have been suffering through for decades. I can only hope that enough of us force ourselves to see and face them together. I hope that the bankruptcy will leave us closer to whole and make it possible for all Detroiters to have a chance at a normal, functioning city.

CHAPTER
NINE

FALL DRAPES OVER DETROIT like a thick patchwork quilt, giving a softer shape and color to the city's hard edges. In the summer the boulevards that radiate out from downtown, running four and six lanes deep with traffic, can seem inhospitable to human life. A few shrubs and scraggly trees are the only protection against a sky that blazes white hot, magnifying every flaw, from cracked sidewalks to potholes, some so deep they are stuffed with shopping carts as a warning sign for passing motorists. But in the fall, as the sun retreats, everything that seemed so harsh now softens. This tough, machismo city becomes gentle and intimate, more human.

The squirrels are out in force this morning, foraging before winter comes. In Ann Arbor they are all fat and happy, little roly-poly bundles waddling through the land of milk and honey. But here in Detroit they are lean and scrappy. They eye Maddie as we walk down the street, taking her measure, taunting her. In Ann Arbor they wouldn't dare; they just chattered at her from the safety of the trees. These squirrels, I think, are city squirrels, and it feels good to be back in a city.

A year after we moved to Michigan and five months after deciding to call Detroit home, we are finally here. If Ann Arbor was a culture shock, Detroit feels like a homecoming. Karl woke up giddy this morning, vibrating with so much excitement that I could feel it as I opened my eyes. Leroy, too, was ready, standing at the edge of the bed, snuffling under the covers, trying to pull them off me. Even Maddie, who likes to sleep in, was sitting up and staring at me expectantly, ready to begin her Detroit life.

The only thing that would have made our arrival better is if we were living in Matilda. But despite the herculean progress of the past few months, there is still too much to be done for us to move in yet. The walls are still wide open as the plumbers and electricians finish running their pipes and wires, and the dirty work—installing insulation and drywall and refinishing the floors—still needs to be completed. So we put all of our belongings in storage and rented a furnished apartment in Midtown through Airbnb. It isn't cheap, but it was the only option that would accept all the animals and offer us flexible dates. We hope it will only be for a few weeks, a month tops, but we want to leave ourselves options.

Cal was thrilled by the news of our delay. He doesn't want us to move into the house any sooner than necessary because, he says, "Clients always have the best of intentions, but once they're living in the space, it's hard. The best of relationships get strained."

I'm not sure whether he meant me and Karl or us and them.

The Midtown we see this morning is an awkward beauty. She's

not what we saw just nine months earlier when we started visiting, but she's not what she will be in just another year either. What she will eventually fully develop into—and for whom—is still uncertain. But we're excited to finally be here, to start figuring out what our place will be in this city. We already feel more at home, on our first morning, than we ever did in Ann Arbor. Just walking the dogs here is different. In Ann Arbor people would cross the street to avoid us, even as I'd call hellos and announce that the dogs were friendly. This morning Maddie already has a circle of fans all petting and cooing at her on the patio of Great Lakes Coffee while we order inside. Leroy is nudging people with his giant Rottweiler head, trying to convince them that Leroys need love too.

I breathe a sigh of relief.

Maddie has always been a good litmus test of towns. In places where I will feel comfortable, she is an advance team, acting as an icebreaker to potential friends; in places I won't, people shun her. I like to think Maddie buys me some street cred. The fact that I don't have a pug or a lab tethered to the other end of the leash is a signal that maybe I'm not a hipster gentrifier coming to ruin the neighborhood. Because everyone knows gentrifiers don't walk pit bulls, right?

Coffee procured, we leave for the West Village to check in on Matilda. It feels like we're driving through a Vermont postcard. The trees flaunt their new coat of many colors, the rust, persimmon, and burnt orange contrasting against a sky that veers between cerulean and sheet metal, depending on the mood of the weather gods. The bushes are on a mission to upstage the trees, glowing an intense scarlet. A flock of a hundred birds alights in an open lot, taking a brief rest as they make their way south. Even the abandoned, trash-strewn buildings have a certain charm now.

Today the sun sparks off the water in the Detroit River like the arcs off my dad's welder. But on rainy days moody skies meet moody waters to create a wall of melancholy. As we drive past, I can see the canopy of trees that covers Belle Isle, a 985-acre park rooted in the Detroit River, right in the international crossing between the United States and Canada. Detroit is the only city in America where you look south onto Canada. In the evenings the vintage streetlights that line the MacArthur Bridge flicker on, a few burned out to remind you that you're in Detroit. When the evenings are cool, thick white clouds of steam billow out of the manhole covers, an eerie veil that blinds drivers and conceals what might be lurking within. Karl and I quickly learn to drive carefully through these pockets of steam because homeless men and women sometimes stand inside them to stay warm.

This is the season Karl and I love more than any other. We can stop dashing from shadow to shadow, crossing and recrossing the street to find shade and avoid the cruel gaze of summer. My childhood memories are filled with severe sunburns and giant blisters, despite my mother's best efforts to keep me lathered in sunscreen. She, like me, has fair skin, a complexion that has only three shades: lobster red in summer, ashen in winter, and alabaster the rest of the year. My father, who tans easily, found our extreme whiteness amusing. I can still hear his laughter ringing in my ears as my mother and I would walk out of the house wearing shorts. He'd flip his aviator sunglasses down from his head and declare, "The glare, the glare! You're blinding me with those legs!"

My mother would shoot him a death stare. Neither she nor I wear shorts to this day.

As homeowners, however, Karl and I are learning what our favorite season really means: raking. Endless raking.

When we arrive at Matilda, we see all of our trees denuded, all of their brightly hued leaves piled up in drifts on our front walk and lawn. Up and down the street it's the same story. Karl and I vaguely remember this from childhood, but our recollections are more about jumping in leaf piles than about the responsibility of raking and bagging. But it's a responsibility we're excited by today because the task is something at Matilda we can actually do. Plus, we don't yet know what leaf-raking etiquette might be, and I don't want to be the house on the block that everyone gossips about because we failed to rake our leaves correctly.

"Hey, Amy," calls Whitney, Cal's daughter, as she sees me getting out paper bags and leaf rakes. "I can do that. I can rake. You two don't need to bother."

She comes around to help.

"That's okay. We can do this," I tell her, possessively guarding my rake.

Four hours later I'm still raking, and Whitney keeps offering help. The blisters on my palms say I should have taken her up on it. But I'm nothing if not stubborn, and I'm committed to removing every damn leaf from our lawn. The maples, of which we have many, dumped an ungodly number of leaves, but at least the leaves are large and rake up nicely. The locust tree, however, is a bitch. The leaves are fine and slim and weave themselves between blades of grass so that they are immune to the talons of my rake. I'm just OCD enough to consider, if only half-heartedly, using tweezers to pick every last one of them off our lawn. Their anemic yellow bodies mock me as they twitch in the wind. It's a satisfying feeling staring across a carpet of green at the end of the day, the leaves ensconced in their biodegradable paper bags, awaiting trash pickup.

I'm congratulating myself as I round the corner of the house, looking for Karl in the backyard.

I stop short.

There is a lake of russet and gold four times the size of the front lawn. There are seven trees—one a dreaded locust—all of which have gleefully shed their leaves.

Another day, I decide, *another day*.

Maddie, however, thinks this is the greatest day ever. She runs through the fallen leaves just like a kid, flopping on her back and lolling about with violent joy until she spots a squirrel invading her yard. Then she flips over, crouches as low as her nine-year-old knees will allow, and starts silently stalking her prey. Meanwhile, Leroy has claimed the front stoop and lays on the top step flat as a pancake, his black fur hot even in the cool of fall.

This memory will be seared into my mind, my last great day with my beautiful Leroy Boy. Less than a month after we arrived in Detroit, and four years after we found him, Leroy will be diagnosed with cancer. His weight will drop precipitously until we can see every rib on his body. He will barely be able to climb the stairs to our second-floor apartment, and then not able to at all. We will have to carry his frail body up and down, if we can even get him to show interest in life. We will be devastated to lose him, a giant hole left in our lives. Even Maddie will come with us to the vet's office when the day comes, a last chance to say her good-byes to the great dopey one. But on this glorious fall day he is happy, a Detroit dog.

While I've been tackling the leaves, Karl has been preparing to deal with a more ambitious project: our garage. We've basically ignored the building at the back of our property since the day we first toured Matilda. We knew it was back there, lurking, but we'd decided to keep this Pandora's box closed. We purchased the house without so much as looking inside. Sometimes it's just best not to know. *We'll deal with it someday*, we told ourselves.

There have been a lot of "somedays" in this project, but Karl has decided that today is that day.

I find the garage charming from the outside. With the faded red paint flaking from its wooden walls, it leaves the impression of a poorly peeled Easter egg. I want to save it rather than replace it if we can, but that decision will be made sometime in the very distant future. Today we just want to assess what we're dealing with.

Karl sees me staring at the lake of leaves and calls me over to where he and Christian are standing. We take a collective breath and Christian pulls out his screw gun, the key to our garage. There is no door, merely a plywood board screwed into place. He hands us the screws as they come out and then removes the board as if he's opening a tomb. We peer into the blackness.

Karl turns on his iPhone flashlight app and steps inside, beckoning us.

The floor is calf-deep in cat litter boxes and bags of petrified trash. Ancient furniture is strewn about. Musty, moldy books are stacked in the corner. I'm certain this is the final resting place of at least a few squirrels. I am thankful for the limited visibility because it means I can't see whether anything alive is scuttling about. If we excavate deep enough, I think, we could find Jimmy Hoffa.

We pry apart the old sliding doors, and the building floods with light. It really does seem like the place was last used as someone's trash receptacle. The books in the corner look promising, even if all the pages are stuck together. A typewriter sits in the rafters, and I wonder whether it's the same one Arthur Herzog once used to type out his menus. I can't quite reach it, though, and am a little terrified to wade farther in to find out more.

"Karl," I say, "this one is all yours. I'm going back to raking leaves."

I return a few hours later to check on him, and though it looks like he's barely made a dent in the debris, the construction dumpster tells a different story, brimming as it is with the remains.

He places the plywood back over the door and starts screwing it back on.

"Someday," he says. "We'll get to this someday."

◆ ◆ ◆

Right now we have to get ready for Stacy's first visit to Detroit. One of the advantages of living here versus Oakland is that Detroit is an easy ninety-minute, up-down flight from New York, allowing Stacy to travel back and forth every few months. During my fellowship in Ann Arbor she came often enough to be an unofficial member of the cohort.

This weekend she is coming for the Guns + Butter pop-up dinner I finally scored tickets to attend after several attempts. Chef Craig Lieckfelt had recently hosted Anthony Bourdain at one of his dinners, and since then it had become the hottest ticket in town. Everyone raves about his deconstructed "eggs + bacon" served inside an eggshell. The plane ticket costs more than the meal, but Stacy wants to see Detroit and how it has changed in the decade since she and I vacationed here together.

Detroit is awash in pop-up fever. Every weekend, it seems, there is a new chef serving a clandestine meal. It's like the raves of yore: buy your ticket, and then wait for instructions about where to go. You never know if the dinner will be in somebody's house, an abandoned fire station, or the middle of a field. These meal events aren't technically legal, as they lack the official sanction of the Detroit Health Department, but they are a sign of the innovation and enthusiasm for food bubbling up in a city that's best-known culinary tradition is the Coney dog: hot dog covered in chili, mustard, and onions. And restaurants are only one part of the pop-up scene here. Retail stores are popping up, yoga studios are popping—everything is popping up. But unlike in New York or San Francisco, these aren't performance art or temporary seasonal shops funded by deep-pocket labels. In Detroit, restaurateurs and wanna-be shopkeepers use pop-ups as a "proof of concept," a way to prove to neighbors, parents, bankers—everybody—that a market exists in Detroit. With very little capital investment, they can test the waters, hone their craft, and build their brand before committing to a permanent location. Light and nimble is the new Detroit way. Even the mighty Detroit Economic Growth Corporation, which is best known for helping the big guy, has a program to bring pop-up entrepreneurs into abandoned neighborhood retail corridors as a way to rebuild outside of the golden bubble.

In the past several months Karl and I have already attended a half-dozen of these dinners, executed at varying levels of accomplishment. And even though not every meal has been a winner, I like supporting these entrepreneurs and being a part of a vibrant food scene filled with faces who are excited about Detroit. I've become a staunch advocate for two nonprofits, FoodLab Detroit and the Build Institute. I've become good friends with Devita Davison, who runs FoodLab, and April Boyle, who runs Build, and these two ladies are among the most amazing, dedicated, brilliant women I have ever known. They are building a vibrant scene of entrepreneurs and small businesses dedicated not just to opening restaurants and the almighty dollar but also to a just and fair food system that gives women and people of color access to the same tools and training that are typically reserved for high-tech, high-growth firms. In a city where I'm discovering that the women just flat-out kick ass, these two are among my heroes.

April—yes, that April, who sent me to Matilda—has graduated nearly six hundred students, many of them African American women, from Build's training programs. She gives them the basics of how to build a business, not just sell a skill. Many of her clients go on to start food businesses and work with Devita and FoodLab to specialize their knowledge and gain access to commercial kitchens. Eventually they may work with Forgotten Harvest, a local food pantry that launched a for-profit incubator to help these small firms grow and scale their products. It's a beautiful network that fosters success and collaboration, and it's having such success that other cities are looking to replicate Detroit's model.

In America today there is a cult of entrepreneurship that says anyone can start a small business at any time and be their own boss. But that is so far from the truth in a place like Detroit, where the poverty level is rampant and failure isn't just something to pivot off of like in Silicon Valley. Here failure doesn't mean starting over; it means not feeding your family. My upbringing makes me understand this on a gut level and cringe at the privilege of people who glibly espouse the doctrine of "follow your dreams" and "fail fast." Yes, do those things, but there is also nothing wrong with a measured approach. Not everyone has the same cushion behind them. But April and Devita are giving training and assistance to those who want to take their ideas and turn them into legitimate businesses that not only are profitable but also employ Detroiters. And that's a significant achievement: fewer than 20 percent of all small businesses across the country actually employ anyone but the owner. And if Detroit is going to truly rebound, it must create jobs.

"Food sits at the intersection of so many social justice issues," Devita says. "If you can help people start their own business and help them grow and scale, they have enough money to feed families. We tell people we are business advocates, but in reality we use food as an inspiration to touch on so many other issues. Food brings people together like no other sector can."

I can't wait to share all of this with Stacy because a passion for food has been the backdrop of our relationship. She introduced me to oysters, taught me about sushi, and always orders the wine. I gave her green chili and bourbon and am still trying to convince her that tomatoes are, in fact, edible. Some of my most memorable and magical meals have been with her. To celebrate my divorce from Sean, we went to New Orleans, where her favorite chef cooked us and a few other girlfriends a private dinner at a table tucked up in the eaves of his restaurant. I cannot tell you what was on the menu, only that we ate for what seemed like hours and that it felt decadent and magical. The evening has a beautiful gossamer quality in my mind and remains one of the highlights of my life.

I wish Stacy had been here to share one of my most magical Detroit experiences thus far. Shortly after we arrived, Donna Terek and Paul "PJ" Ryder invited us to a flash mob–style dinner party called Dîner en Blanc. We didn't know what to expect, but we couldn't believe our good fortune to be asked along.

Karl met Donna and PJ at PJ's Lager House during one of his solo explorations of Detroit the previous fall. Since then, PJs has become our new Bait & Tackle, a staple of our life. And we're not the only

ones who would say that: this beacon of music, booze and camaraderie is the first port of call for many newcomers to Detroit, despite
being a humble dive on a desolate stretch of road halfway between
downtown and hipster-central Corktown and not at the epicenter of
either. But the Lager House's rock-and-roll pedigree—it has hosted
Detroit musical royalty from the White Stripes to Melvin Davis—
draws people of all ilks to its front door. That front door, however,
can be a bit intimidating because the building is a windowless box.
If you're going to find the community and camaraderie that comes
with PJs, you have to be willing to pull open the front door and face
the unknown.

When Karl pulled open that door the first time, he found a cast
of locals all perched at a long, expansive bar, which has hundreds
of multihued guitar picks epoxied into its surface. At one end sat
PJ Ryder, Detroit's unofficial welcoming committee, his long silver
ponytail and bellowing laugh making him a distinctive figure in
town. He and Karl struck up a conversation, and PJ made Karl promise to come back again and to bring me so I could meet his wife,
Donna, the multimedia columnist for the *Detroit News*. We've been
friends ever since.

We couldn't have known then that they would be our spirit guides
through the great Matilda adventure. But as soon as we tell them about
what we've done, they are with us in solidarity. They did their own
gut renovation project nearly two decades ago in Indian Village—and
had a fire destroy their work midway through—so they have plenty
of stories to tell and empathy to share. We will spend so much time
on these barstools, both in need of guidance and relief, that we'll joke
we're a line item on PJ's monthly income statement.

So when Donna invited us to something outside of the bar, we were excited to go. She instructed us to arrive at Dîner en Blanc wearing white, preferably formalwear, and to bring our own table, chairs, and place settings—all in white—as well as a dish to share, preferably white as well. Other than that, she couldn't tell us anything about the hush-hush pop-up dinner. Nobody knows who organizes it or even where it is being held until the night before. There are similar events in Paris and New York, and I wonder what it will be like in Detroit.

Hundreds of people were already setting up their tables under the hot August sun when Karl and I arrived at the field where the Detroit Tigers once played. The grassy lot surrounded by a chain-link fence betrayed no evidence of its glorious past, although an American flag still waved in the outfield. Everybody was kissing and greeting each other as they spread white linens over folding tables and set out candelabras and fine china and crystal. It was like the most eclectic, chaotic picnic ever, stretching out across the infield.

Our contribution was more homespun, cobbled together with what we were able to rummage from the end-of-season sale at Target. I made mental notes, planning for another "someday" when I'd have all the necessary accessories to organize an elegant table.

I saw Donna approaching, stunning in a full-length formal satin gown.

"Salvation Army," Donna told me conspiratorially. "I'll show you around to the best spots."

I was a little underdressed in a white peasant blouse and jeans, but Karl more than made up for that. He had found a white painter's onesie at Cheap Charlies and was wearing it with the zipper pulled down, his chest hair peeking out. With his thick beard and orange-rimmed aviator sunglasses, he looked like a Bee Gee.

Donna pointed us to where she and PJ were setting up and then was engulfed into the crowd, the consummate Detroit party hostess. I want to be her.

We popped a bottle of champagne and then greeted the few people we knew and watched the party around us. I actually felt a little lonely even as I was surrounded by a sea of people. I wondered how long it would be before we could come to an event like this and know everyone, be connected, feel at home. I know it takes time. Friends like Stacy don't happen overnight. Red Hook didn't happen in a few weeks. But intellectually understanding this truth doesn't change how hard it is to start over. I've always hated this part, midway between two lives, the one you've left and the one you're joining. You don't have the benefit of hindsight to know you made the right choice; you're only filled with questions and doubts, especially when you're taking the place purely on faith. We didn't come here for jobs or family or any of the normal reasons you move somewhere. It's not like when I went to New York and a job drew me in, giving me safe harbor. We're here solely based on an idea that Detroit is the community for us, the place our future needs to be rooted in. But an idea is just that—we have no evidence it will prove true.

As darkness fell on Detroit, sky lanterns floated overhead, the heat from their candles propelling them ever higher. As each one lifted off, it added to the collection of giant fireflies silently gliding toward the heavens. The beauty and magic in the Detroit air was arresting. As we watched the lanterns take off overhead, I silently wished for reality to quickly catch up to what was in our hearts.

Having Stacy here at the Guns + Butter dinner makes it almost true, almost real. The night has the same magical quality as my divorce dinner and Dîner en Blanc. I can't tell you what we ate other than the "eggs + bacon," which were divine, but the night itself felt perfect. We sat at a long table with twenty other people all interested in and passionate about Detroit, some from the city and others from the suburbs. Stacy is a source of curiosity, however. Our dining companions are astounded she would travel from New York for a dinner in Detroit. They wanted to hear her impressions of the city, and it's hard not to get enthusiastic as the white wine goes down, the candles glow, and the golden shower of day fades into black outside the door.

"Stacy," I tell her as we walk back to the apartment in the cool night air, "you might as well just move here now. You know I'm always right about these things."

CHAPTER TEN

"I READ YOUR COLUMN regarding your Georgian home in the West Village," pronounces the disembodied male voice coming through my phone. "I'm a forty-seven-year-old life-long Detroiter, never gone anywhere else. Let me tell you, I don't know much about you, but get out while you can."

I pause the recording there and find my latte and donut, a morning ritual purchase from Trinosophes, a café down the street from my office at *Crain's*. I like stopping in on my way to work because the owners, Joel and Rebecca, play the best morning music—a mix of Motown, jazz, and blues, all on vinyl—and tell me stories of the artists and their connections to Detroit. It makes me feel cultured, worldly, like I know more about music than my one record—Dad's copy of C. W. McCall's *Black Bear Road*—might imply. And they do caffè sospeso at the counter, so I often buy a coffee and a donut in advance for the homeless guy who comes in during the afternoon.

Caffeine in hand, I'm ready to finish listening to the message. As a journalist, I get a lot of calls like this, sometimes kooky, sometimes angry, but always entertaining. Everyone tells you that you must develop a thick skin to make it in this business, but I never have. Each comment on a story, each angry voicemail, bites. People don't expect that of me. They think, because of my do-what-has-to-be-done attitude, words don't wound. But they do—even the words of complete strangers.

"Wait until you get kids and try to raise kids in the city like I did," the voice continues. "All these young folks, they want to give them medals because they are moving downtown. You got a lot of us, ma'am, who have been raising kids, and it ain't no picnic. And wait until those homeowner's insurance bills keep going up, your auto insurance. I tell you it's hard to love Detroit when you live in it. You're going to be gone when you have kids, just like all the other young ones who have come and gone. I've seen it for the last twenty years when they all came in with me. I'm the last man standing, and I gotta be here. So don't make my mistake. Enjoy your home now, but keep looking. Just a little bit of advice from someone who knows."

No name. No phone number. No way to call this man back and find out his story. He's trying to help, to give me fair warning. But the call makes me angry. I seethe for days.

When I tell PJ about my drive-by voicemail, he just laughs. "You've just met your first Detroit Hater," he says. "Enjoy. We even have a song for them here, it goes like this," he says as he walks away singing, "Ain't no hater like a Detroit Hater because a Detroit Hater don't stop. Detroit Hater don't stop.'"

I laugh, but the man's comments still reverberate: I know there is truth in his words for so many people who have believed in Detroit before and gotten burned. We haven't lived through the hard times yet. We haven't felt what it's like to watch your dreams turn to ash in the foreclosure crisis or in slowly dwindling services as your neighbors move away and you're stuck or stubborn. We've never had to face the heart-wrenching choice of our kids or our community. I'd like to think we'd choose to get involved with the schools right here rather than moving to the suburbs, but it's easy to think noble thoughts when you don't have to actually test the waters. And we never will. Neither Karl nor I want children.

Don't get me wrong, I love children. There is nothing better than being an auntie to a whole passel of kiddos. But that doesn't mean I want them. I've known since Matt was born *exactly* where babies come from, and it ain't no stork. Dad was gone fighting coal fires and there was nobody to watch me, so Mom had to take me to all of her Lamaze and La Leche League classes. She would send me out of the room for the most graphic videos, but I still saw and learned more than enough. To this day I joke that childbirth is some seriously unnatural shit. Or that all they do is pee inside you for nine months and then take all your shoe money.

It's easier to joke, to make people believe that you would be a horrible parent, than face their judgments or insistence that I don't know my own mind. It is easier for people to think I hate children than it is to explain that I value my career more than motherhood. In my world, kids were something that trapped you and prevented you from achieving your dreams. Growing up, I never knew a woman who had it all. I didn't know anyone who was a mom, fully present, in the way my mom was, and also at the top of her career. Sure, maybe I could get a nanny. Or marry a stay-at-home husband. But I didn't exactly grow up in the kind of place where I'd even know those things were possibilities. All I knew was marriage, babies, cashier at the City Market. If I wanted to get out, kids would be an obstacle, and I didn't want them bad enough to find a way to overcome the challenges.

But my caller doesn't know I don't want kids. He's just assuming and ascribing to the conventional wisdom that says families flee at the first positive pregnancy test because the Detroit public schools are so abysmal. To stay would make you the worst kind of parent. But despite all the haters saying it's not possible to raise kids in the city, that's not the truth in our neighborhood. The sound of laughter, emanating from children riding their bikes down the street, mixed with the thump of a basketball is the white noise of summer. Not even our generators could drown it out at times. Jim Boyle and Mary Trybus, for example, are making an active choice to stay because they want this life and experience for their three children. They've stuck it out even as their friends got pregnant and high-tailed it toward the suburbs. When Jim's own brother headed north of the Eight Mile Road border with his family, it was a gut punch for them all. One family, two different choices.

I don't deny that many of the schools here are bad; that would just be naive. You can't just chuck your kid into the nearest option and call it a day. But there are good schools in Detroit—it just takes more work to find them than most people are accustomed to. Some kids go to private school, some to public school, and still others go to charter schools. But there is evidence everywhere that kids raised in Detroit's public and private schools can, have, and will do great things. Bryan Barnhill, who is the chief talent officer for the City of Detroit, grew up in one of the roughest sections of the city but took his public school education all the way to Harvard. He spent a few years in New York City and then decided to come back and be a part of rebuilding his city. And he wasn't the only one. His high school running buddy, Adam Hollier, came home too. The son of a firefighter and social worker, Adam went to Cornell University before returning to Detroit and getting involved in politics. There is Michael Evans, who dropped out of Wayne State University but helped build a mapping technology that is the foundation of Detroit's efforts to eradicate blight. There is Lauren Hood, who is hosting conversations between longtime Detroiters and newcomers to tell the history and build relationships of trust where there had only been divides. There are Kirk and Tamika Mayes, one of the city's power couples. He grew up here and now runs Forgotten Harvest, a nonprofit that works to eradicate food insecurity. And he convinced Tamika, a high-powered New York attorney, to move to Detroit and marry him. Now she's one of GM's leading lawyers. And, of course, there are Cal's children, Christian, Whitney, and Hailey. To me, they are evidence that great kids are being raised in these 139 square miles, even if the Detroit haters want to pretend nothing good grows here.

I can't get the caller out of my mind as the November elections roll around. Detroit is electing a new mayor and city council, and I'm excited to cast my first ballot as a Detroiter. The stakes are incredibly high. No vote has ever felt as impactful to my day-to-day life because this is the team we have to entrust with our future and with solving the cancerous problems that eat at this city. They are the ones who will have to lead us out of the gilded halls of bankruptcy court and show the world that Detroit can address public education, get the lights turned on, the garbage picked up, blight busted, and cops and firefighters on the street. Because whereas the court can help the city restructure its debt, our elected officials are the ones who must lure more middle-class families back into the city, find ways to help the poorest among us, and ensure that there is a place for everyone in Detroit's future.

The morning of Election Day I drive to the precinct in the pouring rain and prepare to cast my ballot. My choices for mayor are Mike Duggan and Benny Napoleon. Duggan recently moved here from the suburbs to run for mayor, while Napoleon is a longtime Detroit cop and current Wayne County sheriff. Duggan is white but seems to have a broad coalition of support; Napoleon is African American and seems to be relying on the fact that he's a household name. Duggan was a county prosecutor known for tough-guy tactics and the former CEO of the Detroit Medical Center; Napoleon has a law degree and was the city's top cop under a previous administration. They are both Democrats. The rap on Duggan is that he's an operations guy; he likes to get under the hood and really understand what is happening. He is also known to have little patience, quite a temper, and a ready-fire-aim style.

As I stand in the voting booth filling in the bubble, I hope I am making the right choice for Detroit's future.

Our personal future, however, must wait.

Despite our best efforts, we must postpone moving into Matilda. Again. We'd hoped to be in by mid-October. Then by Election Day. Then Thanksgiving—and we can already hear that deadline whooshing by. But we can't wait much longer. We can't keep paying for construction and apartment rent. So we tell Cal and Christian we have to be in by the New Year, just two months from now, regardless of what shape the house is in.

The good news is that Matilda is no longer just the empty carcass of a house. All of the plumbing, wiring, and ducting have been installed, and insulation snuggles around them inside the wall cavities. The south wall is completely rebuilt, crews are starting to hang drywall, and all forty-six windows are installed. It's amazing how a few sheets of glass make us feel like we own an entirely different house. The living room is now glaringly bright. I'd always pictured this room as a dark, private corner, perfect for curling up with a book. I worried that it wouldn't get enough light and would feel like a hole. I never imagined that when the boards came down and the new windows went in, the room would feel so open—and exposed. It almost feels like people walking down the street are right in our living room. We're definitely going to need curtains if we don't want everyone watching *The Good Wife* and *Longmire* with us. Overall I am starting to see how we are going to live and what Matilda will feel like, but there is still a long way to go. The only working toilet is the ancient one Karl found in the basement—and it still has to be flushed with a bucket of water because there is no running water. We have heat and electricity, however, so progress is happening.

I corner Cal and Christian to ask for a favor: Can they quietly make Karl's piano room a priority? I'd like to bring his Baldwin out of storage and surprise him with it for Christmas. We've already agreed not to exchange gifts—the house is going to be our gift to each other for a long time to come—but I want to do something special for Lovey. He misses playing, and I know having it will make all of the stress and chaos more manageable. They agree, and it becomes our little conspiracy. I can hardly wait for Christmas Eve, our first holiday in our house, when we'll unveil it to him.

Because we can't move in for Thanksgiving, we decide to go back to New York and spend the holiday with Karl's family. The entire clan is descending upon his brother, Greg's, house in the Hudson Valley. Even his mother and father, long-ago divorced and remarried, will be in attendance with their spouses. I wonder if my mom and dad will ever be together in the same room again. It will be my first holiday as a full-fledged member of the Kaebnick family, as a wife and not a girlfriend, and I can't say I'm not a little bit intimidated. His family has always been warm and welcoming, but it seems different once you are legally bound to someone. Will they be mad at me, I wonder, for eloping with Karl instead of hosting a big wedding? Do they blame me for spiriting him off to Detroit rather than making a life in New York, where it was easy for both Mom and Dad to visit? Do they think I am good enough for their son? The family is very well educated; even Karl's grandparents went to college. So I fret.

Under the best of circumstances Karl and I both find family visits stressful. Not each other's, mind you, but our own. We both feel under the microscope, on edge, and defensive, even though that's more about our issues and insecurities than their judgments. One of the biggest fights of our relationship happened over something trivial, something I cannot even remember now, while sitting on his mother's front porch in Tennessee. I might have just been hungry. Or maybe he was irritable. I just remember the fight causing all of my fears, insecurities, and uncertainties about our future to come tumbling forth as we sat on those steps.

"Fine," I said to him as I stood up from the porch steps. "I'm done. I can't do this anymore."

There was a pause as Karl looked at me, stunned.

"Are you really breaking up with me on my mother's front porch?" he asked, the absurdity of the situation evident in his tone.

As the blood rushed back to my brain and my anger subsided,

I realized I did, in fact, sound pretty ridiculous.

Sometimes I still can't believe I lived to tell the story—and that Karl still married me.

But if I could break up with my future husband during a casual vacation, I wonder what this more formal experience will be like. We're both a little terrified that his family won't understand our decision to move to Detroit and will spend the Thanksgiving meal grilling us. It makes no sense—his dad has already offered us financial support for the project, and his mom has been enthusiastic. But uncertainty remains because we're getting used to hearing Detroit get beaten down. It seems like the city is always the butt of somebody's joke, and we're already starting to get a little sensitive about it. I'm defensive on Detroit's behalf after just four months living here; I can't imagine what it must be like to have endured this for decades.

But Karl's family is truly thrilled for us and just wants to hear all the tales of the city and the house—the beauty marks and the warts. They were already converts, ambassadors for the Motor City merely because members of their family had decided to call it home. We are touched. What they really want to know is the same thing everyone asks us: Where do you buy groceries? They are under the misguided belief—the same one Karl and I once had—that there are no grocery stores in Detroit.

People assume we can't buy food here because, until Whole Foods opened over the summer, there weren't any national chain grocers in the city. But the reality is that although some areas of the city are food deserts, where residents are forced to subsist on whatever they can cobble together from party stores—a lot of candy and pop, very little green and leafy—much of the city is blessed with a gluttony of options. There are three grocers between our house and downtown alone. The southwest side, in particular, is home to several fantastic markets, including our favorites, Honey Bee Market and E&L Supermercado. We hit Honey Bee for its cheap produce and bulk beans, while E&L has a great butcher and a spicy salsa verde I crave.

On Saturday mornings we go to Eastern Market, a large public market where you can buy your basic farm-stand fare—tomatoes, lettuce, kale, corn—as well as lamb, pork, beef, and other meats that are slaughtered and packaged in the surrounding warehouses. Plus, we like to stock up on our favorites from local food producers: Vietnamese chicken links from Corridor Sausage Company, apricot Darjeeling jam from Beau Bien Fine Foods, buckwheat chocolate chip cookies from Sister Pie. The almond toffee from Dave's Sweet Tooth is like chocolate crack, so I have to avoid it unless I want to eat an entire twenty-ounce jar in a sitting.

The Market, which has been open and serving Detroit since 1891, isn't just a pretty farmer's market, though. This is where the "dirty, nasty business of food" still happens, explained Dan Carmody, its president, one morning over breakfast. He's intense and passionate, a no-bullshit guy, a lot like my dad. He's committed to making healthy food accessible and affordable for Detroiters and to assisting the emerging crop of food producers become part of the economic foundation of Detroit's resurgence. His district is getting a reputation as a hotspot for art, dining, and retail, but he wants to ensure that there is a balance between these sexy consumer businesses and the slaughterhouses and other companies that are essential to feeding the city, even if the public would rather not think about them.

Karl's mom says she wants to see Eastern Market when Matilda is finally done and she and her wife, Linda, can come and visit. But as a leader in the Episcopal Church, a psychotherapist, and a crusader for social justice, she is curious about Whole Foods.

"How can Detroiters afford Whole Foods?" she asks. "If the city is so poor, who can afford it?"

"Well," I say. "It's complicated. But that's the answer to almost every question about Detroit."

The fact is that Whole Foods is packed at almost every hour it's open. The shoppers are black and white and Latino; some are wearing hijab, and even more are wearing scrubs because they are on their lunch break from the nearby hospitals. Some people are very excited about Whole Foods and the fact that a national chain is willing to invest in the city; they see it as a sign of growth and prosperity to come. Some are just glad to be able to have the same services and amenities as our middle-class neighbors in the suburbs. We, too, can buy the free-range chicken and exotic yogurts not found on the shelves of the grocery stores near our house. But others are frustrated because they see gentrification and fear it is a sign of new wealth to come. They, like Karl's mom, wonder whether Detroiters can actually afford to shop there. They see Whole Foods as a symbol of a Detroit that isn't for them, a Detroit they cannot afford.

I understand both sides. I'm a shopper who has the means for Whole Foods, but I wasn't always that lucky. Every time I go in I'm reminded of my first visit to a luxury grocer and how out of place I felt. I was eighteen and filling in for a friend at her nannying job. The mother picked me up and took me to Wild Oats, a precursor to Whole Foods in Colorado, to buy ingredients for her five-year-old son's dinner. From my first step inside I was disoriented. Everything was in contrast to the grocer I was familiar with. There were no florescent lights, no bleach smell. There were friendly signs everywhere talking about the benefits of organics and where the food had been grown. I'd never seen produce in a store that looked so fresh, so ripe. The colors were blinding. As were the prices. I can't remember how much a tomato cost, but I remember thinking my monthly food budget would be blown before I even left the produce aisle.

At Karl's brother's house it looks like the entire produce aisle might be laid out on the Thanksgiving table, which stretches the length of the living room to accommodate us all. The farthest guest is squeezed up to a grand piano in the corner, which Karl and his nieces will play after dinner. It's a beautiful sight, with laughter swirling around us, but it makes me miss my own family very much. This was always Dad's favorite holiday—and mine. Back in Fruita, Mom and I would go to Grandma's house early to prepare the meal. All the cousins and aunts and uncles would come, and we'd play football in the horse pasture as the turkey roasted. If I was lucky, Dad would saddle up Big Red, his giant beast of a horse that stood nearly eighteen hands tall, and take me for a ride.

I've loved that horse since I first saw him on the afternoon Mom and Dad met. Mom and I were in Fruita for a holiday weekend with one of her friends. As we walked onto the property of the people who would become my grandparents, I spotted Red in the pasture just beyond the barbed-wire fence.

"You stay away from that horse," Mom warned me.

Naturally my five-year-old self snuck off, crossing the irrigation canal until I stood before Big Red. I barely reached his flank. He eyed me and snuffled the box of Cracker Jack in my hand. I took out a kernel, pinched it between my thumb and forefinger, and made my offering. I had never met a horse before; I had no idea you were supposed to feed them off an open palm. Red did everything to avoid biting me, curling his lips back, delicately trying every angle to get the sweet popcorn. I felt his breath on my face and the short, stiff whiskers on his muzzle tickling the inside of my wrist.

When he nipped my finger, I screamed. My mother heard it from inside the house. Even though another horse, a more careless horse, might have taken off the whole finger rather than just grazing me, she never forgave him. And Red never really liked her either. He'd buck her off if she tried to ride him. Red and I, however, were inseparable.

Looking at the table, I can't yet spot what dishes are Kaebnick family traditions and the stories that go behind them. I look forward to learning those and introducing some of my own. In the Haimerl family no Thanksgiving is complete without the most white-trash cranberry sauce you can imagine: mix cranberries, grapes, cherry Jell-O, and pineapple together in a bowl and let set. Fill a bowl with marshmallows, cream cheese, and heavy cream, and let it soften in the refrigerator overnight. Whip the creamy goodness together, and serve on top of everything. We call it cranberry and white, and we always double the white and try to forget about the cranberry. To say Karl is dubious about this fine culinary tradition is an understatement. But he's missing out.

I sit listening to the conversations happening all around me until Karl's father, Nick, calls for a toast. He wants to share his thanks and pride in his family, especially the fact that there are three doctors in it: himself and two of his children. Nick is a retired ophthalmologist, Greg is a doctor of philosophy and a published author in the field of bioethics, and Suzanne is a college professor and writer as well. Not to leave out Karl, Nick decides to tell the story of how his youngest came into the world.

"I was the first person to see Karl's cock and balls," he starts, a deep, satisfied laugh resonating.

I nearly choke.

Those are two words I've most definitely never heard before at a family dinner table.

He then recounts the story of how he nearly had to deliver Karl in the family station wagon. They were living out West, and Nick was working as a doctor on an Indian reservation, earning forgiveness on his student loans. Karl's mom went into labor early, and they had a long drive to the nearest hospital. Nick feared he would have to deliver Karl in their station wagon. They made it to the hospital in time—just barely—and the doctor asked Nick whether he'd like to bring his son into the world. It's a touching story, though as Karl's wife, I could live without the cock-and-balls part.

It is a beautiful meal and holiday with my new family, part of the new traditions Karl and I are starting to build together.

◆ ◆ ◆

After dinner Karl and I drive back to Brooklyn to spend a few days with Stacy and see the old neighborhood. We've each been back individually, but we haven't yet faced our beloved, forsaken Red Hook together. When we arrive, everything is the same but different. Our friends are all here, but wearier. Everything looks the same, unless you peer closely at the details. Fort Defiance appears exactly as it did before Hurricane Sandy. You'd have to be a local who knew the very DNA of the place to know a river of sludge and debris had run through here. But we notice. The artwork is rearranged and the bar is set up differently. It feels weird being here and in Bait & Tackle, like we're guests in our former life. It's awkward catching up and making small talk with people who had once been like family. We no longer know all the stories and the in-jokes. We have to face how quickly the tectonic plates of our worlds are shifting.

We drive to the park behind the Red Hook IKEA to throw the ball for Maddie, just as we had on so many mornings before. I liked to come here and watch the waves and admire the sea cranes overlooking the Erie Basin. On fall afternoons we'd come and fly kites, the dogs chasing after us as we ran along the edge of the water, trying to achieve liftoff. Being here makes me think of Leroy.

"Hey, do you see that?" I ask Karl.

There are about two hundred metal shopping carts just standing in the parking lot.

"How have they not been scrapped?" he asks. "There's a scrap-metal facility less than a half-mile away . . . you could just push them there."

"Yeah."

Detroit is a place where anything that's not bolted down will quickly disappear. You just get used to that. And here, all over Brooklyn, lies easy pickings for smart thieves. We realize we are becoming Detroiters: we can spot potential scrap at a hundred paces. Walking through the Red Hook Community Farm where Karl once volunteered, we notice the newly installed solar panels. More importantly we see the copper wire.

It becomes a joke between us, a Detroit version of "I spy."

I spy with my little eye . . . copper wire hanging from a telephone pole.

I spy with my little eye . . . shopping carts by the dozens.

I spy with my little eye . . . sheet metal left unattended on the sidewalk.

I spy, I spy, I spy . . .

We decide we're allowed to joke about scrapping; after all, we're paying the very hefty price to rebuild a house that was cleared out by scrappers. It's better to laugh than to cry.

We get in the car and point it toward Detroit. Homeward bound.

CHAPTER ELEVEN

WE STAND ON THE SIDEWALK looking at Matilda. It's just a few days before the New Year, and snow flutters down, leaving a soft coat on everything. There's a thin layer of pristine flakes on the roof, a matte white next to the bright white of the freshly painted eaves and windows. The change in Matilda is remarkable. She no longer slumps, thanks to the work on the eaves and the roof. She seems to stand taller, straighter, stronger, like she could last for another hundred years. I burst with pride every time I drive up and see her standing there with her perfect dentils. It's nice to see public evidence of our love and investment in the house, in Detroit, even in our own marriage. For the past few years we've been defining the outlines of our life; soon we can actually start inhabiting it.

Karl and I pause and look at each other. He squeezes my hand, as he's done so many times before when we've prepared to face something new together.

A bright green tarp covers the front door, snapping in the gusts of wind. Work to restore this entrance is in progress but still not finished, so we walk to the back door. Karl opens it, and Maddie charges through, the first one across the threshold and into our new home.

Karl and I follow her into the kitchen, stamping the snow off our boots on the welcome mat I purchased for just this occasion. We look around at everything both familiar and seemingly so new. It's hard to believe we live here now.

Karl goes out to get the cats from the car, and I fill our new stockpot with water from the sink, preparing to make dinner. I'm giddy. *I am making dinner in my very own kitchen with my very own water running from my very own faucet!*

The kitchen looks just like the Parisian bistro I had in my mind on all the afternoons we spent hunting for just the right cabinets, tile, and light fixtures. The room is one long galley spanning the width of the house. Two-thirds of the space is the kitchen; at the other end is the dining room. Together they make one giant room for entertaining, just like we imagined. At the center of the room is our prized possession: an eight-foot-long, four-inch-thick baker's table that we use as an island. Karl spotted it in the corner of an architectural salvage shop. It was sooty and greasy from storage, but he immediately envisioned it in this room, at the heart of our life. He loved the divots and cuts, evidence of bakers bludgeoning it with rolling pins and cutting into its surface with paring knives. It took four men to lift, and I wasn't sure our tiny Ford Ranger could carry the load. But here it is.

I'm amazed at how well this room came together, considering all the stress and anxiety we experienced while designing it. We first went to IKEA, assuming we would find everything we needed there. But as we hunted our way through the labyrinth of Swedish particleboard, we grew overwhelmed and frustrated. We tried the kitchen center, where you can use the online design tools, but after several hours of trying, all we had was a fifteen-cabinet pile-up on the screen. If I'd had any of those little Swedish fish, I would have thrown them at Karl as we each second-guessed each other and got exasperated with why the other one just couldn't make it work. IKEA is hard on a marriage in the best of circumstances—and this definitely wasn't one of them.

Exasperated, I called my mother. She is the queen of DIY and designed her own kitchen, so I thought maybe she would have some solid advice. She did: call a professional. Their services are free, and they can help you build a room that suits your life, not just one that is functional. This is not a time to skimp or make do, she explained. The kitchen is where you will spend most of your time, and the room will define so many of your memories. Invest in the kitchen. Stumble your way blindly through other rooms.

Standing here, chopping bacon and sun-dried tomatoes for the orzo pasta that Karl loves, I am so glad we took her advice. We worked with Kurtis Kitchen and Bath, and within a week our designer, Jerusha, had developed a floor plan that incorporated our baker's table as well as a wall of cabinets that stretch almost to the ceiling. Because the room has windows on three sides, configuring all the appliances and cabinets was complicated. But she found a place for everything, including a double oven we found at a close-out sale, a deep pantry, and pullout bins for the dog and cat food.

No more unwieldy bags stuffed under the sink! We selected quarter-sawn oak doors stained a deep espresso, which gives the impression of a modern farmhouse. The dark color was fresh, but the rich texture evoked a sense of permanency. Green industrial pendant lights, which remind me of my dad, hang over the island. A commercial-grade faucet arches above the creamy white farmhouse sink we bought at IKEA. At some point the backsplash and walls will be covered in white subway tile.

I set the pot on the stove and fire up the gas for the first time. It flames high—higher than I expect—before I can turn it down. The stovetop stands in the center of the room as an extension of the island. Underneath are deep drawers for all the pots and pans we will eventually bring out of storage. Tonight I only have the new stockpot to work with and our old Lodge fry pan that Karl had packed us back in Ann Arbor. Knowing we would eventually have to rough it in Matilda, he set aside what he thought were the essentials: two plates, two bowls, two sets of silverware, a few glasses, our cast-iron Dutch oven and fry pan, a can opener, paring knife, spatula, wooden spoon, coffee maker, barbeque grill (in case we didn't have a stove), bikes, our rather paltry collection of tools, and my grandmother's set of vintage ice cream dishes, both the banana split boats and the tulip sundae glasses. When I first saw the box of glassware, I was confused and annoyed. Of all the things we'd need, I couldn't fathom why he picked ice cream glasses. He doesn't even like ice cream.

"Well, I know they were your grandma's and that you love them. I didn't want to risk them getting broken."

My Lovey.

At the end of the long room is our eight-foot-long zinc dining room table. It is handsome underneath the Edison bulb chandelier we bought from a friend of a friend in Brooklyn. The fixture is a showstopper that everyone notices the minute they walk in, and its dozens of lights shine brightly. It was a luxury we didn't need, but we just couldn't get it out of our minds. So we splurged.

Our appliances are still wrapped in the blue protective film, and the floors are covered in a thick layer of cardboard and brown craft paper that will remain there until construction is completed. I am disappointed we're moving in before everything is finished; I had secretly hoped for a big reveal on our first night in the house. But there's still so much to do—so much that it is sometimes hard to remember how far we've come. Thankfully all of the walls are up and have a primer coat of paint. The floors are finished. Cal and Christian installed the toilet and sink in our bathroom and finished our shower, but the other three bathrooms are all awaiting toilets and sinks. All of the doors and jambs still need to be built, and all of the trim and baseboard needs to be milled and installed. Long lengths of boards are stacked up in the hallways, and the living room is filled with saws, paint, fillers, brushes, hammers, drills—all the tools of the trade. It's neat and organized, but it's still a workroom.

The stairs are still being rebuilt, which is a great sadness to me. I knew we would have to replace the balusters, but I hated learning that the banister—the one that connected me to Nona— also had to be upgraded. The height wasn't to code, and the long, buffed railing was cracked and marred. But instead of trashing it, Cal suggests we install the banister along the stairs to the attic— my office—when we get to that phase of the project. So at least Nona is still with me.

The piano room has plastic sheeting hanging from the doorway,

an attempt to keep the dust out of Karl's Baldwin. He was touched
and surprised when we unveiled the piano on Christmas Eve. He
never even suspected anything. Cal and I had been terrified he'd ask
why there was a very large object covered in plastic and blankets
in his piano room, but Karl never even noticed. I've never been so
thankful for his spaciness.

While dinner simmers, I make up our bed with a bright red
quilt and sheets and put our clothes in a junk dresser we bought
off Craigslist. I place one of the lawn chairs we bought for Dîner en
Blanc next to Karl's side of the bed, trying to offer somewhere to sit
other than the mattress. This room, this bed, will become the center
of our lives—where we eat, sleep, read, work, everything. There is
simply nowhere else to just "be" in the house. The kitchen, after our
first night, will become a staging ground for the ongoing work, with
contractors coming in and out. Gary, who is working on our doors,
shows up every morning at precisely 8 a.m. And when I get home,
Cal and Christian are often here in the kitchen, going over plans.
Thankfully we've all become such good friends. Otherwise morning
coffee in my bathrobe could be awkward.

As I walk back downstairs I notice the stack of doors and wainscoting that Cal and I rescued from the First Unitarian Church of
Detroit earlier this fall. The property owner was planning to demolish the church and told Cal we could have anything inside if we got it
out before the wrecking ball came. When Cal told me about the deal,
I was excited to check it out. Karl and I had been struggling with
doors almost since the beginning of the project. The front door alone
has been a saga. It stands seven feet tall and forty two inches wide
and looks to have gotten in a fight with the wrong end of a hammer.
Somebody just beat the hell out of it and then, to add insult to injury,

glued on faux-historic medallions. It's not pretty. The one redeeming characteristic is the old spyglass peephole that swivels around so you can see all angles. It reminds me of Mad-Eye Moody's eye rotating in his head. We assumed we could just find a replacement door in an architectural salvage shop, but Matilda has the unicorn of doors, and everyone between Chicago and New York had come up empty. So I hoped that maybe we'd strike gold in the church or, at the very least, score a few of the twenty-four interior doors Matilda needs. I'd looked at Home Depot, but even their modest wood doors were $100 each. I don't want to spend $2,400 on ugly, basic doors.

Christian, however, didn't want us to even look. The church was built in 1890—twenty-four years before Matilda—and he knew I would fall in love with its character and with the idea of our house having more history inside it. And although the cost of acquiring the doors would be low, he warned, the cost of retrofitting and installing them was a big unknown. I dismissed him, wondering how expensive it could possibly be.

It was pouring rain on the afternoon I met Cal at the church. I ran from my truck to the building's massive wooden doors, which were protected from the rain by a deep recessed alcove. A homeless man sat on the steps, his damp sleeping bag offering him minimal protection. A great gate scissored across the doors, sealing off the entrance, despite the fact that just around the corner the windows hung agape, letting in wind, rain, and humanity. I wasn't sure what to say to the homeless man as I stood there. We looked at each other and then looked away. I was embarrassed. I didn't have a dollar, a cup of coffee, anything to offer him.

Cal arrived, trailed by the architectural salvage agent who was showing us the place. The agent pulled out a ring of keys and opened the gate as the homeless man watched. We squeezed through the small opening and stepped into a hallway. A dim gray light filtered down from the small windows high above. Trash and debris, including used diapers, littered the hallway. I felt like I was walking into a crypt. I've never liked touring vacant buildings or abandoned places; I feel like I'm trespassing on a history and a life that aren't mine.

We walked deeper inside until we arrived at the sanctuary door. Cal opened it, and I was momentarily blinded by the light that poured out. The room was massive, with soaring ceilings, light coming through all of the open, missing windows. Plaster was falling from the ceiling, though two original light fixtures still swung from thick chains. Paint was peeling from every wall. The bones of an organ lay mangled along the wall. I squinted and tried to imagine the room as a place of worship.

Whatever you want is yours, the agent said, if you can get it.

As we moved deeper into the church, we found signs of residents. A mattress here, clothes there, some in haphazard piles, some folded with great care. I was overwhelmed with emotion as I thought about what it must take for someone's life to be reduced to squatting in a church. Blankets were neatly tucked across a dirty mattress before me. A stack of boxes was being used as a dresser. Each drawer was filled with folded clothes, and rows of pill bottles and brushes were neatly arranged on top.

I wanted to leave. I felt like a vulture picking at the flesh of this church, prying into the intimate details of other people's lives without their knowledge or permission. But I pressed on.

The building had no shortage of massive oak doors, each with tall, carved arches. I could feel their quality and craftsmanship in the weight when we pushed them open. Most were graffiti covered and so large that I didn't think they would fit in the house, but Cal assured me they could make them work. As we walked back through the sanctuary, discussing the plan for a crew to come and retrieve the doors, Cal stopped and pointed up at the balcony. The large oak panels featured the same intricate arches as the doors.

"We could use that as wainscoting on the main floor," Cal said.

That would be amazing, I thought. But I was still uncertain. Was it really okay to take these things?

If we don't salvage the woodwork, Cal reminded me, it all becomes rubble. All evidence of a church that has stood for 124 years, erased. Better to take this once-beautiful place and upcycle it to the future.

And here it is in my house. I drag my hand across the doors, tracing the arches, touching the tiny dentils on the wainscoting. These pieces of Detroit history are going to be a part of Matilda, a part of our home. I only wish we'd found a front door.

I'm thankful for Cal and Christian, who have been such good partners. It's almost hard to believe that nine months into this project we haven't had a fight or disagreement, despite the fact that it has expanded far beyond the scope of what we originally intended. Each step along the way we have worked together to make the best decision for the project and our wallets. But we've also come to terms with our limitations. For all of our best intentions, Karl and I are not the people who are going to do the work. We don't have the time or talent. And you pay for the work one way or another: you either pay a contractor or you pay in time and forgone wages. Karl and I are better off going to work each day.

The little girl from Fruita is aghast at that. What happened to her blue-collar roots? But the adult woman from Detroit realizes how far she's come to have this opportunity. And after all the money we've spent putting this house together, the fortune that is already sitting inside the walls, I'm not willing to pinch pennies on what we see every day. We're not installing luxury finishes—other than the wainscoting from the church—but I want everything installed correctly. I don't want to look every day at my very first efforts at laying tile, for example, and notice how uneven the grout lines are or how everything is out of square.

Other Detroiters, of course, are making the opposite choice. All around us other couples in the West Village, like our friends Nick Assenmacher and Ellen Barrett, are rehabbing houses themselves. Each day Nick comes home from work and decides what project to tackle that evening. Sometimes you'll find him trying to run electrical, other times painting, as he makes slow, consistent progress. But many nights we also find him sitting on his porch, exhausted, drinking a beer and wondering what he got himself into. I tell Nick that we're embarrassed at the luxury of having Cal and Christian and that we feel awkward watching the progress on our house while they are inching along. But Nick says he would trade places in a heartbeat.

"You guys are the Joneses," he says. "You're what we're all looking to. The quality on your place is unreal. You shouldn't be embarrassed. You should be proud. Cal and Christian are amazing."

But I also watch what he's doing and am amazed. I love that we're all coming together, no matter how we're bringing life back into these old houses. We sit on drywall buckets and at makeshift tables, swapping stories of our lives, some here in Detroit, some from New York, Seattle, or LA. We all talk about our houses, pulling out our phones to show off Instagrams of progress. We're in it together, these houses pulling us toward each other. We're a community. Newcomers and longtime Detroiters. White and black. Those with money and those who are DIYers. All of us making our way through a bankrupt city, looking toward the future and trying to figure out what it holds.

I bring bowls of steaming pasta up the stairs to the bedroom, where Karl is still getting the animals settled in. I crawl onto the bed, and he sits in the chair. We turn on the TV and pull up the finale episode of *Treme* on HBO. It seems anticlimactic now, but at the time it felt so good, so right, to just sit together in our own home, happy and warm, doing something as simple and normal as watching our stories.

◆ ◆ ◆

Our first houseguest is, appropriately, Stacy.

Cal and Christian hustle to get her room ready, cleaning out all of the tools and debris so we can vacuum the brown paper and set up an air mattress for her. We put up a tension rod in the doorway so she has some semblance of a door. But the bathroom is still a ways off; she'll have to use ours.

This isn't the first time Stacy has come to visit me in a construction zone. Thankfully she's a great improviser. Stacy loves to tell the story of how she once catered a party for a hundred with just a toaster oven. She's not being entirely hyperbolic.

When I was living in Denver, Sean and I hosted an art opening for an artist we'd met in New Mexico. Stacy agreed to fly out and help me cater the party. The plan was for her to cook in the warehouse kitchen, but when she arrived, that kitchen was still theoretical. Twenty-four hours before the big party we were pouring the concrete countertops at midnight. That morning Sean was spraying brilliant red paint on the walls. And just hours before the show opened, he was trying to install the appliances. Stacy wisely decided to prep her menu of passed nibbles—dates stuffed with mascarpone, gougères, endive bites with goat cheese, profiteroles—at my mother's and then cook them at the makeshift gallery in a toaster oven propped up on sawhorses. Nobody knew the difference, though, as she passed the canapés on silver trays. If we could survive that, I decide, we could throw a party at Matilda. We might not have a door on the powder room, but at least all of our appliances work.

I invite dozens of people, wanting everyone to meet my best friend, but I also want Stacy to meet our Detroit. I want her to meet Donna and PJ and all of the neighbors who have become central to our lives: Jim Boyle and Mary Trybus, Bob and Carol Rhodes, Mark and Kathy Beltaire, George and Sheila Robinson, Nick Assenmacher and Ellen Barrett, Tommy Simon and Elle Gotham. Because Stacy is a small-business reporter for the *New York Times*, I can't help but want to thrust all of the remarkable small-business stories I'm discovering in front of her. I want her to talk with April Boyle, who found us Matilda and runs Build Institute. I want her to meet Devita Davison of FoodLab. And Martina Guzman, who works for the local NPR station and is also a powerful advocate for the city's Latino community. I want her to meet Lisa Michelle Waud, an amazing florist and entrepreneur and our first friend in Michigan. I want her to meet Vittoria Katanski, who operates the Hatch Detroit program that awards $50,000 a year to a small-business owner who is opening a retail store in the city; Leslie Lynn Smith, the CEO of TechTown Detroit, who is quickly becoming my mentor and adviser in Detroit; and Matt Clayson, who is building up the city's creative design businesses through his work at the Detroit Creative Corridor Center. I want her to meet Matt Naimi, who operates a drop-off recycling facility as a business because the city doesn't offer curbside recycling. I want her to know Tamika Mayes, who chairs our local community development corporation, and her husband, Kirk, who runs the Forgotten Harvest food pantry. And Alexis Wiley, the new mayor's chief of staff and former journalist. I want her to meet Mary Lorene Carter and Jerry Paffendorf, whose company, Loveland Technologies, developed the "blexting" app that is the backbone of Motor City Mapping, a $1.5 million project that will survey and photograph every single city parcel in order to understand and quantify the full scope of the Motor City's blight problem: blight + texting = blexting.

As I make out the list, I'm amazed by the people I've gotten to know in Detroit. I'm particularly blown away by the women who call this city home. It's awe-inspiring listening to all of them talk about their lives and experiences, why some of them never left and others came here fresh. For the first time in my life I feel like a slacker. These are women who aren't just talking about things; they are out there doing things, starting things, building things. In Red Hook I was the one you might follow in a zombie apocalypse. Here I'd just be one of the hordes trailing Mary Lorene Carter to safety. I want Stacy to know them.

"Don't worry, everything is fine," Stacy calls out to me as I come down the stairs.

The smell of something . . . charred . . . is in the air. I can't figure out what could be on fire, as the fireplace doesn't work yet and we're not cooking anything. We ordered tamales and carnitas from Honey Bee Market, wisely deciding that trying to cook would be too much.

"What is that? What happened?" I ask.

You can never trust Stacy in a kitchen. She is a delightful klutz who will dirty every bowl you own just to boil water and possibly cut her hand off in the process. Despite her catering story, Karl long ago banished her from our Brooklyn kitchen.

"Well, it's more of an 'oopsie' situation than an 'eek flames' situation," she says. "I didn't actually burn down the house!"

"Stacy . . ."

"I inaugurated your new fancy double oven."

"What?"

"I preheated the oven without looking inside. . . . I set the owner's manual on fire. But it's all better now!"

What's a party without a few flames?

When we hear a knock on the back door, we know the party is starting. Mark and Kathy Beltaire are our first guests to arrive, and they come bearing gifts. Not only booze but also a beautiful lithograph of a Christmas tree that Nona had given them as a gift. I am beyond touched by their thoughtfulness and generosity. I can't wait to have a permanent place of honor to hang it.

Within a few hours the house is packed with people. Everyone is laughing and talking. Cal and Christian are here, and everyone is heaping praise on them for the beautiful work they have done. Friends are amazed, even in Matilda's unfinished condition, at how lovingly they have rebuilt this house. Several people inquire about their marital status. I am forced to disappoint a few by telling them that Cal is happily married, but others are pleased to hear of Christian's single-guy status.

"You have the hottest contractors," one of my girlfriends, who shall remain nameless, whispers to me.

I later tell Cal and Christian about the comment. Cal is flattered, but Christian is embarrassed. It's the first time I've seen him blush. Whitney tells me her girlfriends all have a crush on him too.

I look across the room and catch Karl's eye. We know exactly what the other is thinking. This is exactly what we envisioned just months earlier when we were so stressed while picking out kitchen cabinets and deciding where walls should go. It seems a million years ago already when this room was just a pile of debris and studs. Now people are gathering around the island, fetching drinks out of our giant farm sink, faces glowing with the illumination of electricity. Our electricity!

Outside the snow is coming down again in big, heavy flakes. Soon the roads will be impassable, and we'll be digging our guests out with shovels, desperately trying to keep up with the onslaught. But right now, safe and warm inside our own house with our guests, nothing matters except how far we've come.

Karl notices my gaze directed outside, smiles, and walks over to me.

"Romance from the sky," he says as he puts an arm around my shoulders and we look out at our guests.

Snow. Our romance from the sky.

I nod, filled with a deep love of my Lovey and our life.

CHAPTER TWELVE

"AMY, WAKE UP!" Karl shouts. "You gotta get out here. Help me find my glasses!"

It has been a long night, and my head just hit the pillow.

"What the fuck, Karl? What is going on?"

"Muzzy is gone."

Oh. Fuck.

I stumble out of bed and fumble for my socks and shoes while Karl goes running down the stairs. I assume he's found his glasses.

"Hurry. Get down here."

I can hear the urgency in his voice, but it's not helping my socks get on any faster.

I rush downstairs and throw my coat on over my pajamas and head out the back door into the polar vortex. The bitter cold strikes me across the face. The windchill factor puts the temperature at nearly 30 below. Detroit is buried under a thick blanket of snow that started just after New Year's Day and hasn't stopped since. Icicles nearly two feet long—deathcicles—hang from our eaves, and I silently curse them and any damage they might do to my dentils. The constant frigid temperatures will stay until March, making this the coldest, snowiest Michigan winter in a hundred years.

I round the corner of the house just in time to see Karl running at me, dragging Muzzy behind him by a leash.

Karl is naked except for black boxer briefs and his glasses, his feet are bare on the frozen concrete.

"Where are your shoes?" I ask. "You're going to get frostbite."

"I didn't have time," he says. "But I had to have my glasses. I was blind and couldn't see a black dog at night."

We are watching our friends' two dogs, Muzzy and Oberon, for the night, and Karl had taken them out to pee. Because it was so cold, he just opened the back door and let them go, thinking they would run into the yard and do their business the way Maddie would. Instead, Muzzy bolted toward the street.

"Can you imagine," I say, "if we'd lost the dogs? Wouldn't that just cap off this night?"

It had been a doozy of an evening.

Craig and Shami, two of our closest friends from Red Hook, were passing through town on their way home from the Upper Peninsula of Michigan, where Craig grew up. It's a ten-hour drive from his hometown to Detroit, then another ten-hour stretch to Brooklyn, so they called and asked whether they could crash with us. I told them it would be cozy quarters and that Stacy was already sleeping on our air mattress, but sure, the more the merrier.

When we met them in the parking lot behind PJs Lager House, I could see the road weariness written across their faces. They'd spent too long trapped in a car with two dogs, their three-year-old daughter, Mahika, and all of Craig's photography equipment. You could see in Shami's eyes exactly how ready for a beer she was. We headed inside and got everyone settled. Craig and Shami revived as Mahika played chase with the dogs around the table. After a couple of hours we decided it was time to head back to the house and get the baby and dogs to bed. We could continue the party there, we thought, gathered on drywall buckets and lawn chairs.

But when Craig got out to the car, he found the windows smashed and everything they owned gone. It was worse than I first imagined. It wasn't just their clothes. Craig had all of his photography gear in the car—cameras, lenses, laptops, hard drives—and it was all gone. Even the air mattress they bought to camp out in our house was missing. Not twenty-four hours after Karl and I stood in our kitchen reveling in the peace and prosperity of our new life, Detroit reminded us not to get too comfortable.

Shami can be a foul-mouthed fireball in the best of circumstances. In the worst she's not somebody you want to cross. Shami once chased a drunk down the street, threatening to remove him from this mortal coil, after he slapped me across the face for reasons that are still hazy. He only escaped her wrath by stumbling into a cab. That was mild compared to tonight. She was outright losing her shit. I hugged her tightly, partly out of love and partly out of restraint, trying to get her to calm down so we could figure out what to do. When a guy at the bar turned around and made some crack about it just being stuff and her needing to "calm the fuck down," I worried that we might have a murder scene on our hands.

I clutched her tighter to me as a trail of "motherfuckers" poured out of her mouth.

Craig was just stunned and in shock.

Stacy, who is always remarkably good in a crisis, flew into action. She called the cops and tried to explain the circumstances. They told us to sit and wait; they'd send someone as soon as they could. Then she found a nearby hotel that would accept the dogs—no small feat—and her American Express points. Meanwhile Karl and the bartender started reviewing tape from PJs's literally just-installed video camera. When they finally found the section of tape and slowed it down, there was a cheer in the bar. Clear as day you could see a black SUV roll by, scope the car, and then take off. About twenty minutes later it drove up again and a man jumped out, smashed the windows, and started unloading all of their stuff. Not satisfied with that haul, the thieves broke into the rest of the cars in the parking lot as well. We couldn't see any faces, but the cops should be able to pull a plate off the video.

We ordered more drinks all around and then we waited. And waited. And waited. We waited for four hours. All night I hoped beyond hope that DPD would somehow prove the detractors wrong, that tonight of all nights they would prove they weren't the joke the rest of the country perceived them to be. But as hour one passed into hour two, I knew it wasn't going to happen. Still, I never expected that four hours and at least a dozen follow-up calls wouldn't pry loose at least one officer to investigate a robbery worth more than $20,000.

When the bartender issued last call, we realized that it was 2 a.m. and we had a baby and three dogs sleeping in a bar. We decided the best course of action was to take Shami to the hotel so she could get Mahika to bed while the rest of us visited the police station. Karl and I agreed to keep the dogs with us overnight so Craig and Shami could deal with the broken window and other logistics without the added headache of walking and feeding them.

We finally dropped off Craig at 4 a.m., having successfully filed a police report and drove home, ready to put this night behind us.

And then Muzzy made a break for it.

In the immediate aftermath of the robbery I'm a little intimidated and scared and angry. I feel violated. Until now we haven't been personally impacted by the crime that we intellectually understand is a problem in the city. But this makes all the statistics—three hundred murders a year and less than half get solved; more than five thousand robberies and ten thousand cars stolen per year—real. I wonder whether we made a bad choice: Did we get what we deserve for moving to *Forbes* magazine's Most Dangerous City? Were we naive to think Detroit is a city like all others?

It's so confusing. The only place we've ever been the victim of a serious crime was in Ann Arbor. Our first weekend there someone broke into our house and stole my purse and our laptops—with the dogs in the house. We had to borrow $50 from a friends' mom who lives there just to get by until our debit and credit cards could be replaced. As crimes go, it wasn't horrific, but it was annoying to be robbed in the type of place people think of as safe, while we've never had any problems living in those areas that aren't considered to be so. So I don't want to acknowledge that I am rattled. I don't want to give credence to the fear-mongering crime rhetoric that surrounds Detroit. If someone were to give voice to what was gnawing at me internally, I'd lash out, reminding them that crime happens in all cities, that it's not unique to Detroit. If Craig had left a car full of gear unattended in Brooklyn or Denver or Philly, it would have disappeared too. It's an unfortunate situation, but this is the risk of cities, not an indictment of Detroit. I mean, honestly, San Francisco has more car thefts per year than Detroit, and Chicago sees more homicides. Of course, we have fewer people than those cities, so our per capita crime rates are sky high. But I'm still constantly watching over my shoulder, double-checking the car, in the weeks after their visit.

When people hear Craig and Shami's story, they frequently assume the robbery happened because Detroit is bankrupt. They think Armageddon occurred the day the city filed for Chapter 9 bankruptcy protection. They think the cops didn't come because the police force was disbanded as part of the filing. When reporters come to town to talk about what it's like to live in a bankrupt city, they assume we are Mad Max and the city is Thunderdome. They see the phantom streetlights and deep potholes as signs of the bankruptcy. One young reporter thought the hospitals were closed down and people were dying because of the bankruptcy. We could create a drinking game out of all the false reports and impressions about what it means to live in Detroit while it goes through bankruptcy.

The truth is, our cops and hospitals are functioning as well as they ever were. Our streets are plowed as well as they ever were. Our streetlights are on as well as they ever were. The problem is that "as well as they ever were" in Detroit is a pretty low bar. We're dealing with the effects of years of declining population, declining property tax income, corruption, indifference, and ineptitude. Half of the city's streetlights are out because the copper wire was stolen out of them and there was no money to replace the poles or the lights. Garbage doesn't get picked up reliably because, well, the city is broke and doesn't have the money to repair or replace its trucks. The city is blighted because there is no money to tear down the abandoned properties or enforce tickets against negligent landowners. There just is no money and a whole lot of debt. That's the cause of the city filing for bankruptcy protection, not the result of it.

"You have to really love it here or you'd just move to a functional city," says Mary Lorene Carter, who is the closest thing I have to a Stacy Cowley in Detroit.

Mary should know. She grew up Downriver, a collection of communities just south of the city that are known for being more blue collar and industrial, a sharp contrast with most of the suburbs, which are affluent communities. She has watched her city struggle for years and has stuck by it through car thefts, muggings, and more. She was with us the night Craig and Shami got robbed, calm and cool. Her car got rifled too, but she, like us, had left her car doors unlocked. We'd all rather not have a thief break our windows just to discover that there's nothing inside. These are the lessons of not just Detroit, but of city living, whether you're in Chicago, Brooklyn, or LA. Even Craig would tell you he knows better than to leave anything in his car. Mary and her partner, Jerry, could easily relocate their lives and their company to the Bay Area and be nearer the investors and talent. Their chief technologist lives there; Jerry moved to Detroit from there. But Mary says she stays because this is home, and she can afford to make a life and pay her more than twenty employees a living wage. So although Detroit may sound like Armageddon from the outside, from the inside there are seven hundred thousand people just living their everyday American lives.

When people ask what it's like to live in a bankrupt city, I tell them Karl and I go to work, come home, work on the house, play piano, read, hang out with friends, deal with the recycling. He has started brewing his own beer, even though we can barely cook in the kitchen. It's something he's never done before, but he wants to try something new, to reinvent himself, to make something in this city of makers and doers. Every few weeks he spends an evening brewing and bottling batches of Matilda Brown and Nona Stout. At first I'm uncertain about this project—how can we take on one more thing?—but as I watch Karl happily muppeting to himself like the Swedish Chef and going about the production process, I am filled with love for my husband. He loves Detroit, every part of being here, and he is blossoming in this city. It's so satisfying to watch him take the evidence of that, his homebrew, to parties and share it with pride.

Once a month we try to have some kind of silly or fun date, to keep the pressure of construction and everyday life balanced. We make a date out of the People Mover, the train that loops around downtown Detroit. We hop on and hop off, enjoying snacks or a cocktail at places along the route. We enjoy a drink at sundown from Coach Insignia, which offers sweeping 365-degree views of the city from high atop the main tower of the Renaissance Center. We pop in for wings at Sweetwater Tavern. We enjoy salsa-dancing lessons at Vicente's Cuban Cuisine. We walk down to visit the Fist and then over to the waterfront, where we sit and watch the lights of Canada twinkle on the river.

Some weekends we visit the Detroit Institute of Arts and spend hours sitting with Diego Rivera's monumental murals, which are still as fresh and alive to me as when I visited them the first time with Stacy. On Friday evenings we like to come and have a drink in the museum's Kresge Court, one of the city's most sophisticated yet welcoming gathering spots. There are more gilded rooms in Detroit, but few that inspire me the way this space and this museum do. The courtyard is flooded with natural light, and the surrounding walls make it look like you're sitting inside a medieval castle. I once saw a photograph of the space from 1960 in which an elegant young woman sits in the courtyard, smoking, her jacket jauntily draped over her shoulders and ropes of pearls spilling down her chest. It's the kind of photograph that makes you want to be that person, live in that moment. The room feels like the spirit of Detroit.

Come spring we'll start collecting our weekly CSA share from our friends Ryan Anderson and Hannah Clark, who run ACRE, one of the city's many urban farms. Afterward we'll drive up the street to see Sarah Pappas to pick up our weekly bouquet from her Fresh Cut Detroit flower farm. Sitting with Sarah on the shaded, misty grounds, watching the fireflies and drinking in the beauty of this hard, messy city, will be one of the highlights of my weekly routine. It will seem silly to have flowers and the weird vegetables and greens that invariably come with CSA shares in the construction zone that constitutes our house, but it will bring me joy to see all of the bounty on the kitchen island, a reminder of the places and people we gather it from.

◆　◆　◆

"C'mon, Lovey," Karl calls to me. "Come recycling with me. We need to get out of the house."

The house seems so empty after our first action-packed week that we're both feeling at loose ends, unsure of what to do with ourselves.

I feel like we're ghosts living among the saws, tools, and boards. We think about embarking on a project to move the house forward, but we honestly don't know what to tackle. Everything seems both so far along and so far away from completion. Karl vacuums the paper on the floors daily in a valiant but losing effort to fight the construction dust. I wish I were a winter sports girl, someone who would get out and enjoy the weather, but I just want to hibernate. The snow is piled up in thick drifts that are turning black from dirt and exhaust. In Colorado the skies burn brilliant blue all winter long, quickly warming and burning off anything but a major blizzard. Here, though, I come to understand the definition of "low winter sun." The skies stay gray and oppressive for weeks on end, and the snow doesn't melt until May.

Compounding the oppression is my decision to quit smoking after more than twenty years. Well, not so much decided to quit smoking as decided it's too damned cold to go outside and smoke. I had my last cigarette of my last pack on the night of the robbery. I remember standing outside in those below-zero temperatures, sucking down that last cigarette, and thinking, *What kind of insane person am I?* During the renovation I've become a pack-a-day smoker, but I'm typically more of a social smoker. I have always had a hard time separating the twin vices of booze and nicotine. But as one freezing cold day has turned into another, it's become a competition between me and myself to see how long I can stay off the cancersticks.

Getting out is a good idea.

I bundle up for a trip to Recycle Here, the drop-off recycling facility run by Matt Naimi. This is the only place in town to bring your bottles, cans, newspapers, and other items. Here in Detroit there is not and never has been curbside recycling—though it is finally coming. The city privatized its trash-hauling services last fall, and the new contract promises that curbside recycling will start later this year, but for now Recycle Here is the only option. And, in fact, many of us wonder whether we'll participate in the new program or just keep coming to see Matt every Saturday. What he's built is not just about trash or the environment; it's a place of community gathering and connection. You never know who or what you'll see at Recycle Here.

Karl and I pull up to the 260,000-square-foot warehouse, the bed of our Ford Ranger filled with wine bottles and red Solo cups from the party. Matt is standing in the doorway, leaning back on the heels of his steel-toed boots, hands buried deep inside his Carhartt bib overalls. Nearby a handful of people stand warming their hands over a burn-barrel fire. I breathe deep of the smell of childhood. My dad burned our trash in Fruita, and I'd stand there with him as he and the neighbor, Mr. Bale, tended the fire and shot the shit, as Dad would say. I really want a cigarette, but I refrain.

The unheated warehouse offers little respite from the frigid temperatures. It's negative temperatures outside and negative temperatures inside. Still, more than two thousand people will come through the doors today, stand in the bitter cold, and separate their cans from their bottles, their No. 1 from No. 3 plastics, mail from newspapers from magazines, and toss it all into the appropriate box or crusher. People bring their goods by car, by bike, and by bus. Some push grocery carts down the street. Some are young and some are old. The head of the city's economic development team stands next to someone who is struggling to get by. Everyone comes together here because they are committed to recycling, yes, but also because they love this place and community.

"This is caveman-style recycling," Matt tells me while we sit in his office, where a tiny space heater valiantly tries to breach the cold.

He founded Recycle Here in 2005 after a woman chased him down the street, yelling about recycling, in the wee hours of the morning. She knew he had a waste-hauling service and wondered whether he could help her start a recycling program in Detroit. Matt agreed to put one dumpster outside a nearby bar and see how it went. A decade later he is mostly out of the waste-hauling business and focused instead on Recycle Here. To pay the bills, he runs Green Safe Products, a green restaurant supply company that services not just the small businesses of Detroit but also some of the mega music festivals around the country. The money he generates through Green Safe Products keeps the doors of Recycle Here open and lets him live the life of an entrepreneur and artist focused on building a more sustainable Detroit.

"I like the freedom here," Matt says. "I actually like how screwed up it is. I work every day to help fix Detroit, but if we ever complete the job, I'll find somewhere else to go."

Inside the warehouse Maddie is the unofficial greeter for Recycle Here. She dashes from person to person, saying hi and nosing in the trash. It's too cold to keep her out for long, even wearing her bright pink sweater, which is emblazoned with a sugar skull. Soon she'll be banished to the truck.

Sandi Bache Heaselgrave stands in the corner decked out in thick overalls, scarf, hat, and mittens as she makes pour-over coffees and doles out pastries. We know Sandi from our Red Hook days, when we all went to Coffey Park together for off-leash dog hours. She grew up in the Detroit area and recently returned home with her husband, Andy, and son, Henry, with the intent of opening a coffee shop. They opened a first location of their Red Hook café in the tiny suburb of Ferndale, just to the north of Detroit, but have struggled to find a location in the city. Most of the spaces available are either too large or require too much renovation—or both. But Sandi says she may be close to signing a lease in the West Village, just four blocks from Matilda. Another piece of Detroit serendipity.

Parked along the back wall is a food truck serving up steaming bowls of pho and Thai soups. Detroit, like most major cities these days, has a love affair with the simple foods served out of the back of a truck. But most other cities don't see food trucks parked inside a community recycling facility in the dead of winter. I'd love to show this to my dad and explain to him how the lowly food truck that once haunted his job sites has evolved. Back then they were known as "roach coaches." Today they're just known as delicious. Karl and I order two bowls of spicy, fragrant soup and take them and our coffee over to a quiet spot. We set up lunch on top of a trash compactor, its scuffed orange metal contrasting with the green cilantro and limes that we're doctoring up the soup with. I stop to Instagram the moment: "Still life in Detroit."

"I bring you the romance," Karl says. "I take you on a fancy Detroit date. You don't know."

For some reason Karl likes to tell me I don't know. It makes me laugh.

"I do know," I respond, reaching up to kiss him.

I can't imagine a more perfect date than the one we're having standing in a cold, dirty, smelly warehouse, eating pho and drinking coffee, chatting with new friends, some of whom we know, others we're just meeting. For us this is the epitome of life in Detroit. The city may not have curbside recycling and other services most cities take for granted, but it finds a way to work around the problem, to create something new and beautiful. It hustles harder, finds a way to get by.

Because life must go on, even in a bankrupt city.

We will only live and feel the true results of the bankruptcy once it is settled. Right now there is still so much unknown. Will the Grand Bargain get approved? Will it really be enough to help retirees? Will creditors still find a way to sell off the DIA's artwork? Will the judge even decide that Kevyn Orr's proposal for exiting bankruptcy—the "plan of adjustment," as it is formally known in court—is viable and feasible, both satisfying creditors and providing money for reinvesting in city services?

The good news is that the plan does call for significant reinvestment in police, fire, lighting, infrastructure, and more. And some of that reinvestment will start happening and yielding results before the court case is even settled. When the winter breaks, for example, the new Public Lighting Authority will start installing new lights at a clip of five hundred per week. A new curbside recycling contract will be issued, allowing citizens to have their recycling picked up from their house as it is in most functioning cities. Trash will get picked up too. More cops will be put on the streets. New technology systems will be put in place so that firefighters aren't relying on home-rigged systems for alarms.

For now, though, plowed streets are the biggest sign of what could be to come. This may not seem like much, especially to my friends and family in Colorado, where plowing is a given, but here in Detroit you can hear cheers coming from behind the plows. For the first time in years, decades some say, you can drive on the streets of Detroit despite the heavy downfalls of this polar vortex winter. At first snowfall the new mayor, Mike Duggan, promised every single street would see a plow—and he made good. Mostly. A few streets, such as ours, are too narrow. But that we can forgive. Citizens here are used to their politicians making empty promises, to infighting and inaction, so this accomplishment, as trivial as it may seem, is refreshing for many, a sign that maybe this time the revival is real.

CHAPTER THIRTEEN

FLAMES LEAP OUT OF THE CHURCH in the early darkness of a spring morning. They are angry and red as they fight through the roof and toward the heavens. Smoke chokes off the scene, casting everything in a surreal haze.

Firefighters will arrive on the scene, but they will arrive too late. The First Unitarian Church of Detroit will be gutted, just a red sandstone shell, pointed arches reaching toward the heavens, the roof gone. The charred walls will stand seemingly unmoored by any foundation or structure.

Seeing it knocks the wind out of me. This was the church I'd walked through in the fall with Cal looking for doors. I wonder whether I caused the chain of events that brought this church down. Just a few weeks earlier the local NPR station, WDET, had invited me on its morning show to discuss rehabbing historic homes in Detroit. I told them about all of the love—and money—it has taken to move Matilda from a moldering wreck to a still-far-from-complete home. I mentioned on air that we had salvaged doors from a church on Woodward Avenue that was scheduled to be demolished. I didn't think much about that casual comment at the time because it was my understanding that the church's owner had secured all the permits needed to tear down a historic structure.

By the time I got to work after the interview, however, there was already a voicemail waiting for me: the Historic District Commission was curious what church I was referring to because, as far as the commissioners knew, they had not approved any demolition permits for a church. I called them back and told them what I knew, they thanked me for the information, and then I promptly forgot about the situation.

And then, this morning, just before dawn, the church burned.

It could have been caused by an errant cigarette or by one of the homeless men who were squatting there, trying to cook a meal on an open flame. Or it could be a demolition-by-arson situation. Detroit, which is a town that loves a good conspiracy, is already speculating that it is the latter because the church sits across from the footprint of the new Red Wings stadium, making it valuable land. We'll never know the cause, however, because the Detroit Fire Department doesn't have the resources to investigate. They don't have enough arson crews to review every one of the nearly four thousand questionable structure fires that break out each year.

"Nothing burns like Detroit," arson investigator Lieutenant Joe Crandall once told the *Detroit News*.

Still, I fear that my offhanded comments on the radio are somehow to blame for the blaze. Maybe the owner had secured demolition permits from the Buildings Department but failed to get permission from the Historic District Commission. So when I spoke up and the commissioners discovered that a church listed on the National Register of Historic Places was in danger, they intervened. It wouldn't be unusual in this town for one arm of city government to be unaware of what the other is doing. Or maybe the owner never actually secured the correct permits in the first place, and I unwittingly alerted the authorities. I wonder whether I inadvertently saved the wrecking ball only to bring on the gasoline.

In any case, I am conflicted now about whether we are salvagers or scrappers. We thought we were doing the right thing. If we didn't take the doors and wainscoting—and pay for it—all of that beauty would have just been reduced to rubble. One way or another, it seems. But are we really just vultures picking over Detroit's bones? I don't know how many of Detroit's historic structures have been scrapped by people who come to take their trophy, stealing from the legacy and future of the city. Matilda herself suffered this fate. Still, I feel complicit, somehow, in what went down, like maybe we're part of the problem, one of the many who think they can just come and take from this city because no one cares.

Mostly, though, I am angry. I'm angry that the church was allowed to decay to the point I found it in. I'm angry Matilda was allowed to rot. I'm angry on behalf of an entire city. I am angry that we need to spend a billion dollars the city doesn't have to demolish properties that were left to decay by people who wrote Detroit off, be they banks or investors or people who just walked away. I'm angry on behalf of Detroiters who stayed, who every day are forced to deal with the blight and abandonment and other people's vicious disregard for them and their city. I'm angry that those of us trying to repair these homes, to clean up the sins of the past, are being held responsible for bringing them back to exacting specifications, while nobody seemed to be there preventing the problem in the first place. I'm angry that in a city where trash pickup is still iffy and new streetlights are just starting to be installed, I can get fined by the Historic District Commission for planting a vegetable garden in the yard of a house that didn't have water or electricity when I bought it. I'm angry that officials care about the color of my windows and doors even as the city burns.

I want to scream and shake my fists at the air. Where were the Powers That Be during all of this? Who was watching? Where was the Historic District Commission when things were collapsing? Where were the tickets or fines for those who left the city to rot? Why couldn't our neighbors get any help fighting the battle against a Florida slumlord who bought Matilda and then left her to be stripped and scrapped, to become a neighborhood eyesore and trouble zone? Why, at the very least, aren't properties in historic districts—those that have been set aside on the National Register of Historic Places, such as the church or our house—protected from the scumbuggery that has afflicted this city?

The journalist in me tries to be even and measured, to be understanding and empathetic. To recognize that Detroit is a big city with deep problems and limited resources. *Be reasonable*, I tell myself. How was the city, the Historic District Commission, the county, any public body supposed to fine and fight every property left to rot as they watched a tidal wave of people flood across the border into the suburbs and beyond? Not every burned-out shell of a house was abandoned by slumlord banks and investors who only saw dollar signs in Detroit's cheap real estate and then washed their hands of the city when the balance sheet no longer balanced; real, everyday people also left their homes.

How can I blame residents who lost their jobs and had to make hard choices to leave their homes in search of better services, better schools, and what they thought would be a better life? And what about those who left simply because they couldn't stay and feel safe or keep their kids in school? I wasn't there making those choices, having to live that life in crisis.

How is this broke-ass city supposed to pay for staff to enforce the laws when barely half of the residents are able to pay their property taxes and many are too poor even to pay their water bill? How is the city supposed to be worried about one house or one church slowly collapsing when they are drowning in a sea of them? How can I even think about dedicating resources to worrying about that one house or one church when the police and fire departments are forced to make do with broken-down vehicles because the city cannot afford the basic tools of public safety? What kind of irony is it that in the Motor City the police drive hoopties because they can't afford any-thing better? They have to go begging to foundations and private businesses to buy them new cars and equipment. Who am I to stand here and be angry? Who am I to judge and be self-righteous over the fact that I have to get city approval for my vegetable garden?

So I am angry and also empathetic. Day to day I never know how or what to feel here. This is a city of complexity and nuance. Of beauty and devastation. Of joy and sorrow. Some days I am moved to tears by the simple splendor of a pheasant crossing a golden field, its majestic tail held aloft seemingly in pride and defiance. Other days I want to rage against every way this city is struggling, every way it makes life impossible. Every emotion burns bright and strong, no room for gray areas in this in-between place, my new borderland.

There are no easy answers here. But we have arrived at a time when there seems to be a shift in perceptions of the city. The new mayor, Mike Duggan, is making it his mission to bulldoze through some of the most significant challenges that plague the city, and just five months into his term he is earning a reputation as someone who gets shit done. His tactics don't always make him popular, but his results—snow plowed, garbage picked up, lights coming on—are changing hearts and minds. But as hard as it has been to break through those logjams, it has been child's play compared to his most significant task: addressing blight and putting vacant properties in the hands of people who want to rebuild them. Those who own this city will control its destiny, and Duggan wants neighbors, not speculators, to be the ones in charge.

This spring the mayor launched his Neighbors Wanted program, which is auctioning off two homes a day to the highest bidder. The city owns thousands of properties—some due to tax foreclosure, some due to other causes—that Duggan wants off his responsibility list and back in the hands of owners and on the tax rolls. Duggan promised the city when he was elected that they could judge him on the number of new families who call Detroit home at the end of his term, but he can't make good on that promise if finding and financing a house is as challenging as it was for me and Karl.

"We are moving aggressively to take these abandoned homes and get families living in them again," the mayor said when announcing the auction program. "There are a lot of people who would love to move into many of our neighborhoods."

On a sunny Sunday in May, Cal, Christian, and I go to see the program in action. We drive to the East English Village neighborhood on the city's far east side, where the Detroit Land Bank Authority, the agency responsible for executing the auctions, is hosting an open house. This is near where Karl and I ventured when we first came to Detroit together looking for a piano. But this looks nothing like what we saw then; we had no idea we were so close to a stable neighborhood enclave filled with attractive brick homes.

The East English Village was hit particularly hard in the early 2000s with the one-two punch of the foreclosure crisis and the state relaxing residency requirements for city workers. Until 2000, city employees were required to live within the city limits, and many of the firefighters and cops elected to call East English Village home, making it a solid and diverse middle-class community. But after then governor John Engler signed legislation allowing them to live anywhere and still serve Detroit, the lure of better schools and services enticed many just across the border into the Grosse Pointes and other suburban communities. When the foreclosure crisis hit, it just compounded the problem. Property after property was abandoned along these blocks. And the more foreclosures there were, the lower property values sank. Detroiters began walking away from houses they'd paid $100,000 or $200,000 for but were suddenly worth less than half or a quarter of that price. They could rent for cheaper elsewhere and not pay the sky-high property taxes, car insurance, and homeowners insurance that come with a Detroit address.

And they are sky high: when I first started seeking homeowner's insurance, a large national firm gave me a quote of $4,000 per month. *Per month*. That was a message, not a quote. We did eventually secure a policy, but between that and our auto insurance and property taxes, we pay close to $1,000 a month for the honor of calling Detroit home.

Despite the hurdles, not everyone left East English Village—or the many other similar neighborhoods across Detroit that struggled with the same challenges. Those homeowners who remained looked after the properties when the banks wouldn't, trying to fight off scrappers while also keeping the lawns mowed and the windows boarded. As a result, many of the homes here can be salvaged if the right buyers get a hold of them.

When I arrive with Cal and Christian, we find the streets jammed with people and tour busses, everyone out to see what kind of deals might be had. The three of us tour the dozen houses open for inspection, taking notes on the conditions and what kind of construction budget would be needed for each one. At this point I'm getting good enough at estimating that we make a game of it. I usually come in within 10 percent of Cal and Christian's back-of-the-napkin estimate. Most of these properties are gut jobs like Matilda; a few will only require a lot of elbow grease and patience. Seeing the condition of these homes, I'm tentatively enthusiastic about the program. But based on our experience, I have reservations about how people will finance them.

As the hordes move through, I eavesdrop on their conversations. It quickly becomes obvious to me that most of them have no comprehension of the costs of renovation, let alone the challenges to financing. I hear one family talking about how a particular home is so cheap; it just needs a new bathroom. Meanwhile I estimate that property needs $125,000 in improvements, and that's before I notice that the foundation is buckling and a brick wall is bowing outward. I worry that people are going to bid these properties up, not anticipating the rehab costs, and then get stuck with a home they cannot afford to rebuild.

When the mayor first announced the program, people scoffed and said nobody would be interested in buying houses in Detroit. But demand is higher than anyone imagined: more than a thousand people show up to this open house, and the city will raise $1 million in pledged bids in the first month. One house will crash the auction site as bidding accelerates to nearly $100,000. The winners have six months to rehab the house—nine months in historic districts like ours—or the property reverts back to the city. It's a high-stakes gamble when you're talking about homes that need full renovations, cash is in short supply, and contractors are MIA.

And I am right to worry: out of the original twelve homes auctioned, only two winners will actually close on their sales. Everyone else will walk away either because the project is significantly larger than they realized during this brief pre-bid tour or they cannot secure the appraisal values necessary to get a loan. Those buyers will lose their deposits, and the homes will be re-auctioned, starting a revolving door of properties going through the Land Bank two and sometimes three or four times. In the first year of the program approximately three hundred homes will sell, but fewer than half of the winning bidders will actually take possession. Nearly four dozen homes should be renovated and occupied in that time, but only four will be. And of those four, investors own three.

The mayor, Detroit City Council, area philanthropists, and banks are all trying to find solutions, but they don't come easy when the costs of rehab can be significantly higher than the homes will be worth when finished. For newcomers drawn in by the tale of cheap properties, there is bitterness when they discover, belatedly, how unexpectedly challenging the Detroit real estate market can be. All they've heard is the boosterism—nothing about the lack of financing.

Many of them will approach me, hearing through the Interwebz that Karl and I have embarked on a similar project, and ask for advice.

For months I will provide moral support and encouragement to a woman from Los Angeles, also named Amy. She and her husband wanted to move to Detroit, where they could raise their two children closer to his family. They were prequalified for a $350,000 mortgage in California, so when she found a property in the Boston-Edison neighborhood on the Land Bank auction site, she decided to bid. It had leaded-glass windows and a sweeping staircase, all of the historical details and space they couldn't afford in LA. But the excitement of being the winning bidder quickly dissipated as she began to discover all of the financial pitfalls. Amy will send me long e-mails detailing all the phone calls and e-mails she's sent to lenders, begging for help. She simply had no idea that financing a house here would be so hard. But that is there, and this is here. It will take her nearly a year to finally be approved—and the victory will be short lived. The underlying appraisal value will be a paltry $140,000, far less than the cost of the necessary improvements. With more than seventy windows, she's having the same conundrum I once faced: windows or water. She's not sure why she didn't walk away in the beginning.

This is the dichotomy of Detroit: as much as things are changing and improving, the more they stay the same.

◆ ◆ ◆

I'm so thankful to be beyond the early stages where Amy finds herself trapped and, instead, am edging toward a completion date. It's still only visible in the distance, but at least it's now visible. If this were a movie, you would see the days of the calendar whoosh by as time propels us through the spring and summer months, even as no discernible action seems to happen. And yet so much is happening. It's just slow, meticulous work.

Each morning we wake to the sound of Gary coming into the house at precisely 8 a.m.

First we hear the click of the door closing. Then, in just a few moments, Maddie will register the noise and bolt down the stairs, barking like she's going to kill the intruder.

"Good morning, Gary," Karl calls downstairs at about the same moment Maddie realizes, that just like yesterday, it is Gary. Her vicious bark shifts to a whine as she wiggles and throws herself at his feet. It plays out the same way every morning, Monday through Friday.

Gary is our "door guy" who specializes in fine carpentry. Cal hired him to oversee this phase of the renovation, which involves installing the church doors and wainscoting and replacing the trim throughout: door jambs and casing, baseboards, wainscoting, and window casements. Gary is a perfectionist, and I know we are going to appreciate his craftsmanship when it's done, but each morning when he walks through the door before I've even had my coffee, the project can grow tiresome. It's hard constantly having people in our space. Sometimes I wish we hadn't moved forward with the trim. We certainly didn't expect to. It was a luxury, not a right-now project; it certainly wasn't in the budget. But the house continues to be a puzzle, with each piece dependent on the one before it. In this case the door jambs need to be custom built to accommodate the doors from the church. And the baseboard is dependent on the depth of the door casings. So if we want doors to the bedrooms, it ends up being easier to do everything at once. And because the doors in particular come with so much history and so much personal conflict, I am thankful for Gary's meticulous craftsmanship.

This morning I see Gary looking, almost lovingly, at all of the long trim boards stacked up in the living room, freshly delivered from Public Lumber, a second-generation-owned lumberyard located in a part of town that doesn't incline you to stop even if, like me, you drive a truck so beat up that nobody steals it even when you leave the keys in the ignition. (Truth: I've done it three times.) The neighborhood was different when Christa Sarafa was a child. Her dad would bring her to work, and nobody watched over her; she was free to roam the streets. She wouldn't let kids do that today. But still, Christa, who owns the store with her mom and brother, is committed to staying open—in Detroit—and growing the business.

I love looking around our house and knowing that we're a tiny part of Public Lumber's survival, that there are pieces of Christa and her family in our house. As the daughter of a small-business owner, this type of thing is important to me. I want to know whom I'm shopping from, be able to have relationships with the owners, and know that our business, our commerce, helps them feed their families. This is about more than just a house for me; it's about creating a sustainable community of people who support one another. That's what Dad taught me business was about.

The lumber Gary is eyeing will be used to replicate the balcony Cal salvaged from the church. We are using the gorgeous arched panels as wainscoting in the main hallways of the first and second floors. But we don't have enough to go up the stairs, so Cal and Gary are recreating the pattern, on the angle, to complete the look. Just looking at the massive oak panels leaning against the wall, I can see how gorgeous it will be. But at this point it's anyone's guess when the project will be finished. At first we all thought it would take a few days to cut down the panels and install them. But that's when we were only going to do the first-floor hallway. In reality it will be months before we're done. We're not even asking about cost at this point because we're so far down the road that there is no turning back. We do know it will be expensive. We do know that we don't have enough money. Cal and Christian know that too. They are float-ing us at this point with the assumption that "someday" we'll get a mortgage and be able to pay them back. The project just got away from all of us. The relationship we've built is more like family than business, and, like family, we're all in it together.

I recognize that this sounds crazy. If anyone told me that story, I'd ask if they were high or mental. Whose contractors float them work and money just because they love the project? The personal finance editor inside me is speechless. This is not the foundation of a solid financial plan that leads to solid investments and long-term stability. But the Amy who leaps then looks, trusting that the path will come out before her, believes. When I tell Stacy, she just laughs and gives the classic Detroit answer: "Because, Detroit." It's the answer you give when you can't even begin to explain this city. Sometimes it's meant as gallows humor. Sometimes, as in this case, it's a statement of amazement. "Because, Detroit" means: it doesn't make any rational sense, but you're also not surprised by the fact in question, good or bad, because, well, it's Detroit.

◆ ◆ ◆

"Why did you stay?" I ask Jim Boyle one evening as we sit around a fire in his backyard on one of the first truly warm nights of summer. Karl brought over some of his homebrew to share, and I'm toasting marshmallows with their kids.

"We almost didn't," he says. "Your house was an albatross for us. What was happening with it reflected our lens of happiness with the block."

Before Alison and Fatima owned the house, Matilda belonged to a Florida investor. He purchased it out of foreclosure, intent on making it an income property. But like so many out-of-town landlords, he didn't really care about maintaining the property or even paying his taxes. He rented it out to a revolving cast of tenants who grew progressively less responsible about its upkeep or being good neighbors. The last tenants were a single dad, who worked nights, and his teenage sons.

"One night I went over there with a big smile on my face," Jim recounts. "I said it would be really great if you could turn the music down. They all kind of look at me, their heads kind of tilted down. Nobody says anything. So I'm like, 'Okay, thank you, I'm going to go back to bed now.'"

Two nights later their first car was stolen. A month later their second car was stolen.

Jim and Mary laugh about it now, because what else can you do? They recount the story of Jim chasing their gas barbecue grill down the street on crutches. Or Mary discovering a squatter naked and facedown in a snowbank on Matilda's lawn when she left for work one morning. They are filled with what are now charming stories, but at the time these incidents pushed this couple to put their own house on the market and consider following their friends down the well-worn path to the suburbs.

But they stayed. They just couldn't leave the first house they'd bought together as a married couple, the only one their son, Finn, and daughters, Frannie and Lucy, had ever known. They bought the house in 1999, when everyone thought they were crazy to go to

Detroit, and rehabbed it over the course of years, removing asbestos ceiling tiles, overhauling the kitchen and bathrooms, gingerly stripping the original wood of years of bad paint jobs. They eventually got the exterior a fresh coat of paint, removing all evidence that the house had once been bright pink.

"It was really Mary who kept us here," Jim says. "Plus, we found a school that was really working for Finn. The other thing was we didn't have anywhere to go. We didn't have anywhere we wanted to live. We wanted to be in a city."

"We just loved it," adds Mary. "It is close to the water. And the neighborhood has this sense of history. When we moved in there were all these eccentric characters on the block, and they would tell these stories about the people who lived here, and they were the kind of people I have an affinity for."

"You get this yin and yang, and it's either horrible or awesome," says Jim, jumping in.

The spouses have a well-worn way of adding layers of depth to their conversation without talking over one another. I make a note to learn from them for my own marriage.

"And the truth of the matter is that it's both. When we first moved here, we became buddies with the entire garage-rock scene. All of our friends were in bands. There was such a community that was here. It's so intoxicating. You totally fear going into another community and living these kinds of everyday, nondescript existences."

"It felt then a lot like it does today," Mary says. "The momentum in the neighborhood was similar to what it is now. People were excited. Property values were up."

I think of that conversation whenever I start to get angry about the past or uncertain about the future, when I don't know what to say to Amy. Their story buoys me when I'm frustrated by the struggles so many are facing as they try to construct their dreams in Detroit. I try to remember the Boyles' commitment to this city and block—the commitment of all of our neighbors, really—and use it to keep everything in perspective. After all, they've been here, done that, and are still smiling. I know that all I have to do is walk up the block or stop in at PJs, and I will find a friend who is ready to tell it real, but also with real love. I hope that I, too, can find that balance.

CHAPTER FOURTEEN

SUMMER MORNINGS ARE A MAGICAL time for me in Detroit. During the cool of the day I like to pack up Maddie in my old Ford Ranger—just like Mom and I used to do in Dad's old Ford Highboy—and go for a walk on Belle Isle while everything is quiet and peaceful. Even the buzz of the cicadas is quiet.

Maddie has learned the words *Belle Isle* and rushes toward the truck the minute I ask whether she wants to go. She begins to wag her tail as we approach the bridge to the island. She tilts her nose skyward as we drive across, catching the familiar scents flowing in through the back window. Indeed, she knows this place intimately.

As we exit the bridge and round the corner toward the west, we get our first glimpse of the Detroit skyline on the horizon, where sea and sky seem to meet. On cloudy days the water and sky appear one and the same, a gray mass stretching on to the end of time, punctuated only by the five Renaissance Center towers, home of General Motors. Today, though, the sky is filled with cotton-ball clouds and the river runs a brilliant turquoise. I take a mental snapshot because neither film nor Instagram can truly capture the colors.

We pull over and watch the Scott Fountain come to life, its central spray shooting forty feet toward the heavens. For years the fountain sat silent, weeds popping up in its marble steps, but this year it was restored to glory, its milky white marble so elegant and seemingly permanent amidst the Queen Anne's lace growing wild around it. We drive on, past the carillon, just as its bells begin to ring. A group of walkers waves to us as they pass by. I nod and smile as we continue on.

Maddie's tail thumps ever faster until, finally, we bump across the rutted parking lot at the eastern-most end of the island. This is not the place of family reunions and picnics, of kite fliers and afternoon Frisbee games. This is the wild, untamed part of the park where the grasses grow tall, waving in the breeze, and the trees cluster along the lagoons and the riverbank. The beam from the great lighthouse shines out over the waters of Lake Saint Clair as they flow into the Detroit River, keeping the massive freighters safe as they maneuver the narrow channel.

Most mornings we have the area to ourselves, and we revel in what feels like a stolen moment, the luxury of being alone in the country in the middle of the city. We walk along the path that takes us curving around to Hipster Beach, named for those who flock to it with PBR and barbecues in the evenings. In the summer we come here seeking the cooling breezes, but in the winter I prefer to walk a wooded path on the interior of the island because it is sheltered from the cold, damp winds that buffet the park. Sometimes we spot one of the majestic blue herons that call Belle Isle home. It is a stunning sight, these birds standing peacefully on the frozen river as the woods hush around them.

Maddie wades into the swimming hole, sinking down into the muck until she looks like a hippo, with only her nose, eyes, and ears above the water. She was once a powerful swimmer, happy to dock dive into the lakes of Colorado or swim among the kayaks in the turbulent waters of New York's East River. She would drag out giant tree branches and driftwood that later became the raw materials for artisan furniture makers. But now she's a wader, an ambler, an aging dog who is happy to loll in the grass and take the occasional dip.

Our morning walks together are meditative for me. This is where I come to think and reflect on life here in Detroit. It seems impossible that we've been Detroiters for a year. Time has both frozen and blurred. I feel like my relationship with the city is deepening. I'm moving out of the early romance phase and leaning into the hard work of marriage. And just like with my marriage to Karl, there are some hard times.

When we first arrived, the community was so warm and welcoming. Karl couldn't believe how nice everyone was. But I'm discovering the anger that simmers just beneath the surface. People seem to be on a mission to out-snark each other. It feels, at times, like everyone is cynical and that nothing can be good, no one can do anything right. There's always a gimlet eye throwing shade. I have a T-shirt that reads, "Detroit vs. Everyone," and someone once suggested to me that it should be changed to "Detroit Loves Everyone." But that's just a fucking lie. Detroit is one angry city as it finds itself on the precipice of significant change. The cacophony of social media is deafening and damning as everyone talks about "us" (Detroiters) vs. "them" ("hipsters," "newcomers," "gentrifiers," anyone from New York) and New Detroit vs. Old Detroit.

What am I, I wonder? An us or a them? New Detroit or old?

When we bought Matilda, we saw signs that things were turning around ever so slowly, signs that Detroit might one day be the flourishing city it once was. But today there seems to be no shortage of news about the new restaurants opening and old buildings being reborn into luxury retailers or luxury condos for the young professionals all moving in. Tom Boy, the nasty little market near our temporary apartment, the one where the goods were often spoiled and I'd have to walk through a gauntlet of handsy men to enter the store, is becoming a leather goods store that will sell $400 handbags. Fashion designer—and Detroit native—John Varvatos is opening one of his luxury outposts in downtown. The building cranes fly high everywhere. Meanwhile many of the longtime and mostly black-owned businesses feel pushed out as commercial rents rise. They are angry as they watch subsidies and tax breaks for the newcomers, while there seems to be no help for them.

That's the real fear, if we get right down to it: a cultural gentrification. Incomes and home prices haven't really risen that far or that quickly. Per capita income is still less than $25,000 in the booming downtown and Midtown areas. It's even less the farther out you go. Median home sale price still hasn't topped $20,000. So although there are no longer $250 lofts to be had in downtown Detroit and a significant amount of development is happening, we're a long way from the hyper-gentrification of San Francisco and New York. Instead, what we face is the hurt and anger that comes when who is here and where they shop and what they want is changing. The city is still 83 percent African American, but you can walk through downtown and see very few black faces. The halls of political power are diverse, but the halls of economic power are still mostly white. So we wonder what will happen to the Caro's Corners of Detroit. Will they disappear? Will the things that this city valued and loved be shoved aside for me and mine? Or will we learn to coexist together, the new and the old?

Longtime Detroiters tell me they are angry because they feel invisible, like their history is being erased. They want to shout out: *We are here!* They feel like they don't matter, even though they held on when they could have left. They are tired of journalists writing the same story about the same young artists and entrepreneurs who come to make their fortune and "save" this city. They are tired of watching the media whitewash this proud black city. They are tired of those who come acting entitled, like Detroit should be thrilled to have them. That rhetoric is insulting. It pretends that those who are here don't know any better, don't know how to solve their own struggles. They are tired of being forgotten in the narrative of rebirth and reinvestment. They feel like a casualty of the future. They are afraid that this city will finally get its shit together and then turn its back on them, leave them behind. Mostly they are tired of hearing only about people like me and Karl.

Detroit writer Marsha Music encapsulates the frustrations in her poem, "Just Say Hi! (The Gentrification Blues)" published on her website and in the January 2015 issue of *Infinite Mile* magazine. It is one of the most moving and powerful pieces of writing I've ever read on the topic of gentrification and alienation. Unlike so many of the cultural critics in Detroit, she doesn't attempt to out-snark anyone;

instead, she lays bare the emotions of hurt and anger and betrayal.
Here are a few stanzas from the poem:

All around Detroit we talk, from shops to congregations.
There's much discussion of the city's new gentrification
and all the changes with the folks a'moving to the D
the changes in our lifetime thought we'd never live to see.
We talk about The Newcomers, with righteous consternation,
ol' school exasperation, 'bout a disconcerting thing—
"They don't even SPEAK!" we say, when we get on the subject
our mantra of rejection of in-vi-si-bi-lity.
Our indignation hides the sting of truly being unseen,
of being looked-right through—in our own city.
Ralph Ellison, he wrote of this so many years ago.
Walk past and never turn an eye to see us oh! what pity.
Detroit's a place wherein we "speak" to you in varied tones
Hey! Hi! Hello! How ya' doin'? Whazzup? What's happ'nen'? Whaddup Doe!

Detroit is widely said to be a big, small southern town
the separation's one or two degrees, is what we've found
We nod our heads at passersby; acknowledge other folks.
Goes back to railroads underground, rebukes of ol' Jim Crow.
We do affirm and say a word to those whom we pass by
A simple thing but means a lot to us, so

Just Say Hi!

You see, we live on many blocks that seem unaltered by the clock.
With neighborhoods of much good care, of lovely lawns and kept-up yards

and look, with just a camera's twist, it seems as if we don't exist.
But now Newcomers have arrived, our neighborhoods get newly eyed
and even so, for sure we know, how hard we fought to keep our homes
and though we know we were ignored, our labor was its own reward
for our beloved city rests, on many shoulders that were blessed.
We had no time to feel bereft, we carried on when others left

Just Say Hi!

The topic of newcomers and gentrification is a source of strife and discussion with my friend Suzette Hackney, whom I met during the fellowship. As a reporter for the *Detroit Free Press*, she covered the underbelly of this city, from cops and crime to City Hall, and saw firsthand what Detroit is and does to those without the resources to be a part of the great reimagining that Karl and I are included in. She keeps me honest about life in this city, making sure I remember that our Detroit, the one with good jobs and a home renovation, isn't real for most of the city's residents. She has since moved out of the city, on to new jobs and better opportunities, but we still see each other and talk over too many glasses of wine about life in a bankrupt city.

We agree that life is pretty good for those who were already well off and pretty lousy for those who weren't. We acknowledge Mayor Duggan's improvements and that this summer, for the first time in years, every park has been mowed at least twice. Life is improving, at least minimally, across all 139 square miles of the city. But she also sees a Detroit that is getting wealthier and prettier for those folks with money, who are mostly white. She doesn't see anything happening for those who are poor and mostly black.

When Detroit filed for bankruptcy, Politico asked her to write a story about what it means for everyday Detroiters. Her essay reminded everyone that for every story of a me and Karl, there are those "forced to grocery shop at the corner party store for cheap vittles or [who] nearly electrocute themselves because they were trying to tap into a power line to heat their unfurnished and uninsulated shack of a home."

She set her piece in the West Village, where she too once lived. When she visited for the article, however, it looked nothing like what she remembered. There were kids in the streets, people on bikes. Patrons spilled out of the doors at Craftwork, the new restaurant that opened just after the New Year. When Suzette lived here, the scene was different. The faces she saw were mostly African American. There weren't kids on bikes. There was no street life.

"I'm fearful," she wrote, "that in our enthusiastic desire to see one of the world's most iconic cities remake itself into an attractive hub for the tech savvy, the artistic and the upwardly mobile, we're losing perspective of the need for sustainable jobs and an affordable quality of life for the majority of those who don't live in downtown or Midtown and will never have more than a tangential connection to those areas."

If Suzette and I didn't know each other, hadn't established a trusting relationship, we might make assumptions about each other and our intentions. It would be easy for her to dismiss me as another white, entitled newcomer. But I might mistake her as someone who doesn't welcome new people and new ideas, who doesn't want the city to thrive. Both perceptions would be patently false, but perceptions are powerful things in a place that is as defensive as Detroit.

And that's at the heart of my conflict. On the outside I look like a gentrifier. I appear white and affluent. But in my head I am still just a poor girl from Fruita. How can I be a gentrifier when all I did was do all the things I was supposed to? I went to college and got my degree so I could have a better life and build a career. But because I am drawn to places that feel like home, that are blue collar and working class, where communities thrive, I fear that I'm the pariah who brings gentrification. I am part of the new wealth and privilege remaking both our cities and small towns, pushing others aside in favor of our organic, free-range, pop-up, craft-beer life.

So I can understand why people are angry when people who look like me—young(ish), white, and seemingly well-off—arrive in this city and have every opportunity, while its native sons and daughters struggle. But it's hard not to feel hurt and angry. Sometimes I want to lash out: *I am not a gentrifier!* Other times I'm tied up in knots as I search for just the right words and tone to make people understand that I want to be here permanently, not just when it's easy. I don't feel like I'm entitled to have a voice and, if I do, that I'll say something wrong or insult. That I will be judged and found lacking. I feel like I need to apologize for everything. I feel like I have to apologize for finally making it to the middle class. I feel like I have to apologize for having enough money to pay my water bills, while so many Detroiters are getting their service shut off. I feel like I have to apologize for my very being and existence because I am a symbol, even to myself, of everything that others do not have. I feel like I have to apologize for having the ability to remake Matilda from an abandoned house into a home.

It feels as if the mere hint of success makes me irredeemable in the eyes of Detroit. Any success can be suspect here, as people wonder what you did to get it or how you sold out. I get it; it's a poverty mentality. When all you've ever known is fighting for every scrap, it's hard to not see others as the competition for the limited resources. But it still hurts because they can't know when they walk past my house and look in the windows of my life, as I looked into other people's windows all those years ago in Denver, what I did to be sitting here.

I am proud of myself for what I have accomplished and for having the chance to build this life and to choose to do it in Detroit. I know it's not because I'm special or different. It's not because there is anything unique about me. I wish I could say there were, that I could point to one thing about me that says I deserve this more than someone else, more than my brother, but I can't. I got lucky and had good parents who sacrificed. I got lucky and found good mentors such as Donna Ladd, who pushed me at moments when I needed it. I got lucky in so many small ways that got me here, renovating a house in Detroit, trying to make it a home, but looking to all the world like a gentrifier.

The result, however, is that Karl and I don't know where we fit and are often embarrassed by our house, of our life. We don't always know how to talk with people about the good fortune we've had that allowed us to build this home, to invest in this city, even as others don't want to. When friends come over to see what we've been doing, we downplay the work and cost that has gone in. We don't want anyone to feel bad by comparison or for us to sound ostentatious. So many people are proud of our house and the work we've done, the investment in this neighborhood, but we can't quite express it yet. We're still too embarrassed at the idea of having the privilege of being the gentrifiers.

But how can I be one as I watch my family be buffeted by gentrification back home?

Golden, where my family moved after Fruita, was once a blue-collar haven. It wasn't a suburb of Denver but rather its own town with its own culture, set at the base of the Colorado foothills, where the prairie meets the Rocky Mountains. It was one of those places where different socioeconomic groups all lived within proximity of each other. Sure, most of the wealthy lived in bigger homes in the surrounding mountains, but in town all income brackets mingled, shopping in the same places, eating at the same holes-in-the-wall. There was Meyer Hardware and Foss Drug, where you could get a new refrigerator or a six-pack of Coors brewed fresh down the street. Steve's Corner sold you boots and Carhartts. The Ace High was the bar in town, its dark recesses a mystery to me. My dad spent his twenties there, and everyone knew him and my uncles. Need Dick? Leave a message at Kenrows, the local greasy spoon.

But like so many small towns across the West with easy access to the ski slopes, Golden has evolved into a bedroom community vying for those residents who want a home halfway between their workweek downtown and the weekend at the resorts. Expensive condos dot the main street, overlooking the "Welcome to Golden: Where the West Lives" sign. Cheap new construction gobbles up the fields where horses once pastured. You're just as likely to get a $100 bottle of wine as a freshly drawn Coors, despite this being the brewer's world headquarters.

My family no longer feels welcome there. The new residents frown upon their muddy boots and rumbling trucks—all signs of work. My dad and brother don't fit the newcomers' vision of the city as a luxury playground with a small-town feel. Meyers Hardware, where my family had a long-standing account and my brother bought his first rifle, is perpetually on the verge of closing its doors because residents would rather shop at the nearby Home Depot than a third-generation family business. The hundreds of Harleys that once lined the street outside the Buffalo Rose Saloon have been mostly chased out, their leather and loud pipes no longer welcome in town. Kenrows burned down. Golden is no longer a working-class town with working-class sensibilities.

Yet the newcomers tout their redevelopment efforts—and they're not wrong. They've rehabbed a long-vacant department store that squatted on a prime corner of downtown, bringing in a much-needed new tax base. Once-empty storefronts are now filled with jewelers, bike stores, and $12 sandwich shops. Starbucks has a prime location. Tax receipts are up, and tourists are flocking. Home prices are on the rise, fattening up city coffers.

Both sides are right in this debate. My family feels alienated and pushed out in favor of more affluent residents. But the new townies can't rightly see why anybody would complain about new businesses and a thriving downtown. And just like them, I find myself touting the benefits of my arrival in my new hometown. The increased property taxes. The buildings reborn.

So I am both gentrifier and gentrified.

◆ ◆ ◆

I wish I could be falling unambivalently in love with this city, experiencing the joy of it the way Karl does. Maybe because he's not a journalist, not in the thick of the social media cacophony, he doesn't hear or internalize the same anger and fears I'm struggling with. I'm jealous of his pure childlike love for Detroit. It's a beautiful thing to watch. And I think that because he is so sincere, so genuine, nobody doubts him. They can just feel his joy, and it is infectious. It also means that Karl will go anywhere, open any door. His wide smile and bellowing laugh somehow ingratiate him where others might feel uncertain or unwelcome. He can make friends anywhere.

In the beginning it was PJs. Today it's the Elbow Lounge, a bar with a red peeling facade on a derelict, best-be-gettin'-on stretch of Mack Avenue.

We drove by Elbow for months, each time Karl looking at the place longingly, saying we should check it out one night. This is, after all, the closest thing we have to a neighborhood bar— though it's almost fifteen blocks away. I was usually noncommittal, uncertain about the heavy door and gate out front. As a reporter I'll go anywhere, but when I'm off duty, when people don't have a reason to talk to me, I tend to be more circumspect. I like to know what I'm walking into, and this place has no windows, no line of sight.

When I decided to make a weekend trip to visit Stacy in Brooklyn, Karl used my absence as an excuse to go check it out. Within an hour of my departure he'd not only gone to the bar; he'd met the owner and received a standing invitation. It was like PJs all over again.

Karl pulls open the heavy door, and we walk into the dark bar. We're the only white faces here. I look at Karl questioning: *Is it okay? Are we intruding on a private space?*

I'm still getting used to what it feels like to be the minority. Issues of race and class hang over the city, coloring perceptions and interactions. Who can be where? Who is welcome and who is not? I'm a little hesitant to assume my way into new spaces. I want to learn about the culture of this city, black and white, and be respectful.

"Karl!" shouts an enthusiastic voice. A man comes walking toward us, arms out for a hug.

Karl says hi and introduces me to Kevin, who wraps me up too. Meanwhile the other patrons at the bar have already greeted Karl, shaking his hand, asking how he is.

I shoot him a look: *How many times have you been here?*

He shrugs, sheepishly.

This is a cash-only, no-frills bar, not the kind of joint that carries my standard Bulleit Rye, so I ask for a Jim Beam neat while Karl gets a Bud.

"What was that drink you wanted, Karl?" Kevin asks. "Woodford something?"

"Is he trying to get you to carry Woodford Reserve?" I ask Kevin, laughing.

"Yeah, but I can't figure out which one that is."

He pulls out the liquor distributor's ordering book and hefts it onto the bar.

"Look in here and tell me which one to order. We'll keep it on the shelf for you." Then he sits down next to us. "Have I shown you my grandbaby?" he asks, pulling out his wallet. His daughter recently had her first child, and Kevin is beaming. He shows everyone his pictures. You just know this child is going to be spoiled.

Kevin remembers coming to the Elbow with his dad when he was a kid. It was a Sunday tradition, all the fathers bringing their kids to the bar while they came to watch a game or catch up. It was just how it was done. Kevin says he knew from a young age he wanted to own this place; he liked the spot it held at the center of the community.

Eventually he did buy the bar and keeps it open just four nights a week. It's his passion project, his side hustle. His main job is as an obstetrics nurse at the hospital. He has his nursing degree from University of Michigan and has worked at the hospital for going on thirty years.

He loves his work, loves being the only man on the floor, loves those babies.

This is a man whose story should be told, I think. This is the real Detroit. These people and places hidden from the spotlight, living their lives, keeping Detroit proud and alive.

Elbow quickly gets added to our regular rotation of places we visit. We try to get there at least once or twice a month. We like to go in on Thursday evenings, when it's quiet; Saturdays are a raucous party that gets a little loud for me. Everyone who finds out we go to Elbow Lounge is astounded—black and white—and wants to come with us. I expected white Detroiters to have never patronized it, but I assumed black friends in the area would have. But that stretch of Mack seems to be universally disconcerting. Most have always wanted to go but never have, just like me if it weren't for Karl.

"Man, I've driven past this place my whole life and never come inside," said John Eligon, a reporter for the *New York Times*, when I brought him here while he was in town. His grandma lived on the east side of Detroit, and Eligon remembers passing by Elbow, always wondering what was behind the red door.

Karl and I are choosy about who we bring to Elbow, only inviting those we think will appreciate this bar and won't be annoyed that they can't order fancy cocktails. This is Kevin's pride, and we only want friends who will appreciate and love this space. It's not a dive bar or an old man bar or a hipster bar or anything like that. It's just a neighborhood spot where people celebrate the milestones of their lives—including Karl and me. We celebrated our second wedding anniversary here.

Sitting at the bar, I understand that once you get through Detroit's tough outer shell, get to the heart of its people, prove that you belong here, they welcome you. They want you. But you don't get to come just because you said so. You have to earn your way into this city. You have to prove that you come correct, that you are here to participate, to love, not because you want to change this city or you wish it were some other way. Dad always hated all the people coming to Colorado, touting how much they loved the state and its people and customs but then demanding that it change the culture to be more like wherever they came from. If Detroit is going to change, it's going to be because as a city, as a people, we do it together.

We need newcomers—and yes, I say it as we, because I feel like a Detroiter, even if not everyone else thinks I can be. We need money. We need a middle class. We need some wealth. We need people who can pay their property taxes and build a base so Detroit can afford to provide city services, to help pay the costs of providing services for those who cannot. We need people who can afford to pay into a regional transportation system so that those without cars, those who cannot afford the sky-high car insurance rates, have a way to get around. Until we bring some wealth into this city, none of that can happen. We cannot survive, let alone thrive, without new investment and new energy. But we need it from people who come, as Spike Lee would say, with some "motherfucking respect," not at the expense of those who have held on. Detroiters will be cautious. They don't know who is going to abandon them, who will leave. So they put you through the wringer. They make you work for it, earn your way in.

And that's what we're trying to do.

Looking back, I realize I had to work out my own anger at feeling excluded from Detroit to understand that what I was experiencing was hurt. I had to spend a lot of days walking around Belle Isle, trying to process all of my emotions. But it helped me realize that these are conversations that will never stop. Living here, everyone will always be analyzing and debating the future of this city. It is a complex place, not a training-wheel city. And when I made my peace with the process and realized that the issues are about hurt more than anger, I feel like I am finally starting to understand Detroit.

"Amy, nobody ever thinks I'm a Detroiter and I grew up here," my friend Vittoria Katanski will say to me months later when I confess my emotional turmoil as we sit in her backyard, sipping on wine while her son, Frankie, plays in the grass. "They see some white woman and think I'm not from here. And then when I tell them I grew up in Delray, the poorest part of Detroit, they step back.

"I'm tough to navigate. I usually don't like new people. But you are different. You say 'hi' to people; you wave. You talk to people. You take the time to care about people, this city, and what it has to offer. You want to learn it, not change it. You don't just drive into your garage and get out and go inside and ignore what is around you. That's not how we do it here. Many who have moved here now have never lived in a city, have never just said 'hello' to a stranger on the sidewalk passing by and wishing them a good day. We are nice here.

We want nice back. And that is one reason why newcomers are not always welcomed with opened arms: because they take Detroit for granted. They think Detroiters 'broke' Detroit. It must be our fault, and they, in all their wisdom, will 'fix it.' Umm, no people . . . Detroit will be fixed by its spirit and by the love of that spirit from the people that move here. Basically, don't come into a neighborhood acting like a 'fixer.' Just learn. Become a part of the community in which you chose to live. You get it. That's why you're a Detroiter. You love this city for what it is."

CHAPTER FIFTEEN

"AT LEAST WE DON'T HAVE debtors prisons anymore?" Stacy says hesitantly, trying to be funny but unsure of how to soothe me.

I am sitting inside the truck, pulled over on the side of the road, half crying, half screaming, and entirely in shock. On the seat beside me is a package of tax forms from our accountant. The big red number on the first page says we owe the IRS close to $55,000 in unpaid taxes. I can't even fathom that amount. It's so large that it seems surreal, like a joke. But it assuredly is not.

I really want a cigarette. Why, again, did I quit smoking in the middle of a life-changing renovation? That was stupid. I'm going to need to go find a gaggle of smokers and walk through their second-hand smoke. Even a contact high would help right now.

I knew when we cashed out our retirement savings last year that

the taxes we had withheld wouldn't be enough. I was prepared for
that. I was even prepared for the 10 percent penalty the IRS assesses
for early withdrawal. So I have been saving to cover what I estimated
would be a $20,000 bill.

Evidently I wildly underestimated.

I never anticipated that our retirement savings, when combined with
our salaries, would push our household income so high that we would
trigger the IRS's alternative minimum tax (AMT). But we did, one of
the growing numbers of middle-class families to do so. In 2013 the Tax
Policy Center expected 3.9 million taxpayers would be surprised by the
tax, which was created in 1969 to ensure that the wealthiest pay their
fair share. It's affected more and more families in the intervening four
decades because the income level that triggers the AMT has not risen
with inflation. Congress changed that in 2013, as part of the fiscal-cliff
negotiations, but it still wasn't enough to help us out.

"Yes, I guess the good news is that we won't go to prison," I say,
laughing. "What can the IRS do to me?"

In my panicked state my laughter sounds somewhat maniacal.

I shove the papers back into the envelope and push it aside. For
now I'm going to practice that tried-and-true approach to financial
planning: ignore the problem and hope it goes away.

A few days later, when I'm more calm and rational, I open the
package again. My blood pressure rises just looking at the number.
This is no job for a novice negotiator. I decide the smart course of
action is to call a tax lawyer. Maybe we can cut a deal. Maybe, just
maybe, the IRS will look at what we're doing and our finances and at
least waive the AMT. If they do, we could take all of the deductions
and credits I'd been counting on and whittle our bill closer to what
I was expecting.

Wishful thinking.

The lawyers tell us that, no, the IRS is not inclined to negotiate with us. We can try, but we don't have any of the classic signs of financial distress: there is no job loss or medical bills. We have solid incomes and no kids. We don't look like a couple who needs help. It doesn't matter that the money went to rehabbing a house in Detroit. It doesn't matter that acts of financial suicide, such as cashing out your 401(k), are the only way to make it happen here. It doesn't matter that while everyone, including the Obama administration, is wringing their hands and wondering how to rebuild Detroit, people like us are doing it. No, the IRS doesn't factor in any of that. In its eyes we are just rich fuckers who need to pay their taxes.

The irony is bitter. I sometimes wear a T-shirt that Stacy's husband, David, made during the financial crisis that reads: "Shut the fuck up and pay your damned taxes."

I would certainly like to; I have no opposition to paying my fair share. But this seems excessive for the circumstances, and I have no way to do it. The IRS will just have to get in line and wait along with everyone else. The house is almost ready for its appraisal, and I am hoping the valuation will be high enough to pay everyone back, including, now, $55,000 to the IRS.

I wish this was the largest bill I've received for Matilda. But it's not. The largest one was for $92,092.95. I nearly hyperventilated when Christian handed it to me. But at least I was able to pay that one with the final proceeds from all of our varied sources of funds. This bill is entirely different because there is no more money, and the final construction tab is still looming, large and unknown.

When it does come, we will have sunk more than $400,000 into this house—four times our starting budget. There have been some luxuries, no doubt; the bill for the trim alone will be epic. But Cal's original estimation of $350,000 to bring the house back to life, minus those luxuries, was pretty accurate. That's simply what it costs to take a historic shell and rebuild a house inside its walls. It sounds like a fortune—it *is* a fortune. I would have balked at the sum if you told me eighteen months ago that we'd be this deep into Matilda. I'd have said there's no possible way it costs that much. But it does. Dad told us to ask for quality work at a fair price, and that's what Cal and Christian gave us.

Not everyone will have to—or choose to—spend that kind of money on their Detroit houses. But it's more common than people would like to believe. We are not an anomaly. We simply did the work in one long construction jag rather than protracted over years. And I don't regret it. This isn't an investment; this is our home. This is a place and community we are married to, for better or worse.

Still, I'm hoping our appraised value will be significant, because our debt load feels like an anchor. The one thing Karl didn't want when we embarked on Matilda was to become house poor. And that's where we are standing right now. A high valuation would also help our neighbors and everyone who hung on through the lean years, hoping their own homes would one day again be worth at least what they paid for them. Detroit can't thrive if three-thousand-square-foot brick homes like Matilda are perpetually selling for $35,000. So I cross my fingers that, with enough dancing monkeys, we'll get close to a $200,000 value when we go to the bank next month and ask for a loan.

Lest I feel too overwhelmed by my own financial time bomb, I just have to think about the city of Detroit. The final days of the bankruptcy trial are waning, and everyone is curious about how Judge Rhodes will rule. Will Detroit be allowed to exit bankruptcy, shed its debt, and start over? Most of the creditors have signed off on Kevyn Orr's plan of adjustment—even the retirees okayed the deal for the Grand Bargain—but that doesn't mean Rhodes will concur. He has explicitly stated that the court will not approve a plan that puts the city right back in financial peril or places the city's residents in danger of worsening city services.

In covering the trial for *Crain's,* I've developed a little bit of an intellectual crush on Judge Rhodes. He regularly says that he wants the approximately twenty thousand pensioners to come out as whole as possible but that he must also be attentive to the seven hundred thousand people living in the city of Detroit and what they deserve. His rulings are always filled with steel and compassion, even as he's made the kinds of hard decisions nobody wants to be responsible for.

He has allowed citizens and retirees to testify at trial, giving them an opportunity to question the fancy lawyers. And not in a half-hearted way either: when those $500-an-hour attorneys try to be circumspect with the citizens, Rhodes orders them to answer the citizens' questions directly and concisely. To me, that act—which was not legally required—represents the depth of his empathy and commitment to hearing from those who have to live with the results of this bankruptcy. He didn't just leave them on the sidelines as another judge might have chosen to do. Rhodes is like a modern-day King Solomon trying to figure out how to split the baby. He's constantly balancing the competing demands of making the city financially whole so it can thrive while doing as little damage to retirees as possible. That doesn't mean, however, that everyone is always pleased with his decisions. There are frequent protests in front of the courthouse as people express their deep-felt anger and distrust over the bankruptcy. Some quarters don't believe the city was ever as broke as Kevyn Orr presented. Others believe that the bankruptcy is illegal because Orr—not an elected representative of the city—took us down this path. Still more argue that the pensions are protected by the state constitution and should never be impaired.

But Rhodes has proven himself an ally, playing hardball with the banks and bondholders on behalf of the citizens. At one point, for example, he forced the city and two of its biggest creditors, Bank of America's Merrill Lynch unit and UBS AG, to renegotiate a deal, even though they had already announced a settlement that would have allowed the city to exit a bad financial deal worth about $1.4 billion for the low, low price of $235 million.

Rhodes was appalled and demanded better.

"The court," he said, "will not participate in or permit the city to perpetuate the very kind of hasty and imprudent financial decision making" that led to where it is today.

He would send them back to the table two more times before finally signing off on an $85 million settlement.

That process put everyone on notice that he put Detroit's residents first and foremost. But there are no promises of what is to come.

When the appraiser arrives at our house, I'm a ball of nervous energy, both scared and giddy, like a first date. This day has been a long time coming, and this man we don't even know holds our entire financial future in his hands.

Cal is here with us to answer any questions and point out all of the technical aspects of the renovation. I've put together a one-sheet flier extolling Matilda's virtues: three bedrooms, three and a half baths. Gut renovation. Full basement. Finished attic. New plumbing. New heating. New electrical. New water heater. New drywall throughout. New historic windows. Finished hardwood floors. Historic trim and details throughout. New bath and light fixtures throughout. New kitchen cabinets and appliances. New roof with cedar shake on the dormers. New dentils. One mile from Belle Isle; three miles from downtown; adjacent to Indian Village.

I hand the evidence to the appraiser and start chatting him up about what we've done, but it's clear this is a man who wants to be left alone to do his job. Karl, Cal, and I trail behind him as he silently takes notes and passes judgment on our house. I can't help myself at certain points, and I interrupt him to show off a detail I don't want him to miss. I'm so filled with pride as I watch Matilda being viewed through someone else's eyes. I explain the providence of the wainscoting and point out the new dentils. We've just barely finished tiling the attic bathroom and hope he doesn't notice—or care—that technically the bath and sink aren't hooked up to their water lines yet.

For nearly an hour he tours through the house as we all follow him like pathetic Maddie dogs. As he goes to leave, he tells us we can expect to have the report in two weeks. It's going to be a long two weeks.

Whatever number he comes back with, we've already jumped a major hurdle that we couldn't find a way over when we started this project. Talmer Bank and Trust—the local institution that said it might be able to write us a cash-out refi mortgage when the work was done—has agreed to do just that. We've decided to work with Talmer both because they were kind to us in the beginning and because the word on the street is that this is the bank to use if you need to make a deal happen in Detroit. Because it's a local institution, it knows the market. It also doesn't have Wall Street investors to answer to, so it has the ability to meet borrowers' needs while still staying sound and solvent. More importantly for us is that Talmer is known as a bank that can get high appraisal values.

At the time I don't know how it does. Only that it does. I will later learn, while moderating a panel between bankers and federal regulators on behalf of Zillow.com, that it is the result of choices the bank made after the mortgage meltdown. In 2010 Congress passed the Dodd-Frank Act, which changed the rules of how appraisals can be ordered. One of the causes of the crisis was the cozy relationship between mortgage brokers and appraisers. With a hint-hint-wink-wink, brokers could nudge appraisers to inflate valuations to get sales done. To ratchet back on that practice, Congress said that brokers could no longer order appraisals themselves; they would have to go through a lender, such as Talmer Bank or Chase or any bank that issues mortgages. Additionally, neither the broker nor the bank could talk to the appraiser about the properties they were evaluating. The goal was to give appraisers some independence and firewall them off from influence. To implement the changes, banks could go one of two ways: they could order appraisals from a large appraisal-management company (AMC) or they could, essentially, create a separate in-house team to handle the duties.

Most banks chose the first option because it is cheaper and easier. They can just call up an AMC and say, *Hey, we need you to send someone to appraise a house.* Under this system there are no guarantees that the person coming to value your home is familiar with the city, let alone the neighborhood your house is located in. That may not be a problem in places with more stable real estate markets, but it is wreaking havoc in Detroit. The first problem is that many appraisers won't work in Detroit—they think it's too dangerous—so you don't get the best talent making the judgment calls. And when you do get someone, most likely from the far-flung suburbs, they can't tell the difference between solid, stable neighborhoods and struggling areas. As a result, they may value your house against homes that sold within the prescribed radius of your house but that have little similarity to yours or your neighborhood. That means your exquisitely renovated home, a gem of a property, may get values that are extremely depressed, despite what you've invested.

But Talmer chose to keep its appraisal arm in house. Loan officers call the bank's appraisal-management staff, who then hire local appraisers to do the job. The loan officer and the appraiser never get to talk or discuss valuation. That simultaneously ensures the firewall Congress sought and allows Talmer to work with professionals who understand the local market. For Matilda that means they would compare her against sales of similar homes in similar neighborhoods, such as Indian Village or Boston-Edison or Palmer Park, rather than just sales in the immediate vicinity to Matilda. A local appraiser would know that most of the recent sales near Matilda wouldn't be fair comparisons because they are either foreclosure sales or aren't within the West Village's tiny footprint. So we're hoping this will work out for us.

◆　◆　◆

The e-mail from the appraiser arrives just three days before my thirty-ninth birthday. Looking at it on my screen, it's what Stacy would call a Schrödinger's cat situation. Schrödinger's hypothesis is that the cat is neither live nor dead until you open the box; it lives in a state of flux until you take action. It's a wonky thought exercise in quantum mechanics that we like to apply to journalism: the story the writer just filed is neither live nor dead until you open the e-mail. So you want to open the e-mail at the exact right moment and hope the story is "alive." We sometimes e-mail each other with just one phrase—dead cat—when we receive one that is in particularly rough shape.

Today I e-mail Stacy one phrase attached to the appraiser's report: *Live cat.*

A $300,000 live cat.

That's right: the appraiser valued our house at three hundred large. It's better than we even dreamed.

"The subject is at the final stages of a complete interior and exterior restoration," he wrote in his evaluation. "Most owners in this area do not complete as extensive of a renovation as is currently being completed by the owners. Those renovations that are similar are typically not sold, similar to the subject. For this reason, the subject is superior to all sales in condition. There have been no recent or proximate area sales offering a similar quality of renovation."

All of those details that have slowly eaten us out of house and home suddenly prove their worth: a mortgage of $240,000. (The remaining $60,000 is the required 20 percent equity that typically comes in the form of a down payment when you get a loan on the front side, rather than the back end, like us.) The loan will just be in Karl's name because of my foreclosure, but we'll both be on the ownership title. Talmer will use the funds to pay back the loans and credit card debt we've taken out and then issue us the balance to disperse between my family, the IRS, and Cal and Christian. Even though there won't be enough left to cover all of our debts, we feel like we've hit the jackpot.

Three months later the City of Detroit will receive its answer. It feels like we have come full circle: six weeks after we bought Matilda, the city declared bankruptcy; ten weeks after we receive our financial resolution, Detroit's will come too.

On the morning of November 7, 2014, Judge Rhodes will spend 105 minutes—almost two hours—reading his ruling from the bench. At the end, he will confirm Kevyn Orr's plan of adjustment and allow Detroit to exit bankruptcy. "What happened in Detroit must never happen again," he says. "The hardship and anxiety that its employees and retirees, and their families, have endured and will continue to endure must never happen again. This must never be repeated anywhere in this state. What happened in Detroit must never happen again."

Rhodes will allow the city to slash nearly three-quarters of its unsecured debt—about $7 billion—and spend $1.4 billion over ten years to reinvest in the city. The biggest chunk—$520 million—will go toward fighting blight. Another $464 million is dedicated to police, fire, and emergency services both to upgrade equipment and to put more people on the streets. The finance department will receive $145 million, a head-scratcher until you realize the accounting systems were so antiquated that a $1 million check from the school district was once found, uncashed, sitting in an office drawer. There will also be upgrades to the mostly unused city airport, parking infrastructure, and IT systems. In short, there will be a massive reinvestment. Everyone just hopes, in a city like Detroit, where the former mayor is in federal prison for fraud and racketeering, that it will actually be spent where the court has promised it.

The mood in the courtroom that morning will be tearful and congratulatory. There will be numerous speeches as everyone thanks each other for settling in sixteen months—record time for a municipal bankruptcy—what once seemed like an impossible situation. There were essentially no assets and no money to pay creditors. But the Grand Bargain prevented the city from having to leverage its future to pay for its past. Retirees, while still facing devastating cuts, will fare better than was initially feared. Their health care will be decimated in cost-cutting measures, most will receive no cost of living adjustments, and, most brutally, the city will claw back nearly $200 million from their retirement annuity accounts to recover excess interest payments. But their pension checks will take a maximum 4.5 percent hit. It's far from ideal, but it is over. Kevyn Orr will leave his post, returning the city to full governance by its elected mayor and city council. A financial oversight board, however, will stay in place to ensure the books stay balanced for the foreseeable future. The time of reckoning is over; the time for healing and moving forward begins.

"A large number of you told me that you were angry that your City was taken away from you and put into bankruptcy," Rhodes says in his ruling:

You told me in your court papers. You told me in your statements in court. You told me in your blogs, letters, and protests. I heard you. I urge you now not to forget your anger. Your enduring and collective memory of what happened here, and your memory of your anger about it, will be exactly what will prevent this from ever happening again. It must never happen again. When Fredia Butler testified during the

confirmation hearing, she quoted the great wisdom of Marian Wright Edelman, who said, 'Democracy is not a spectator
sport.' And so I ask you, for the good of the City's fresh start,
to move past your anger. Move past it and join in the work
that is necessary to fix this City. Help your City leaders do
that. It is your City.

CHAPTER SIXTEEN

LIQUOR. BEER. WINE.

The pink and green sign—*liquor* in sea-foam green, the rest in melon pink—peeks in my window through the leafy trees that set it off like a frame. There's the pine tree in the foreground, two giant locust trees overhanging the scene, maple trees on either side. If I peer out just beyond, through the foliage, I can see our garage, which looks like a charmingly dilapidated cottage from this angle, and the angry gray of the Detroit River after twenty-four hours of pummeling rain. In the distance I can hear the whine and revving of the Indy cars running the Grand Prix on Belle Isle, an annual tradition that brings motorsports and months of disruption to my favorite park.

I'm sitting upstairs on our bed in our master suite, which was finished last night. After two years of construction, Matilda is finally done—or as done as she's going to be for now. Most of the house still needs painting and lots of little odds and ends finished up, but those are things we can do over time. But in here everything is pristine because, as a parting gift, Christian painted our private space and installed curtain rods. The walls of our bedroom are a soft Navajo white, a calming backdrop for our red sheets and colorful artwork. Our bed sits on a frame for the first time in our relationship. We finally found a platform that met our aesthetics and our price point.

I feel so grown up.

I shouldn't like the sign staring back at me. The lights that illuminate it on the side of the building cast bright beams into our room at all hours. But I do. It's a reminder of urbanity tucked into what would otherwise be a nature scene. I can't believe how much this feels like home, exactly what we'd longed for—even if we couldn't visualize it—when we started this adventure two years ago.

Christian was here earlier today packing up his tools so they can start another job tomorrow. After two years there will be no Cal, no Christian, no Gary in our house six days a week. It is bittersweet. I don't know how I'll feel not having them here in the morning. Already the house feels a little quiet and empty, although in here it is chaos as I unpack all of the boxes from storage, where they'd been for almost two years. It's like an archeologists' dig as I rediscover who I was when we started this process: What did I wear? What did I like? My clothes carry the scent of Ysatis by Givenchy, my signature perfume since high school. I haven't worn it in so long that I'd forgotten it was once the smell of me.

I've found dresses I'd long forgotten about and boxes of boots and heels I am surprised to own. I can't remember ever wearing heels here in Detroit. I mostly wear purple Sorel snow boots in the winter and pink pumas the rest of the year. This woman who has boxes of Cole Haan heels and BCBG Max Azria dresses seems incomprehensible. Could she have imagined sitting on a bed in Detroit, looking out at a pink and blue *Liquor. Beer. Wine* sign?

I think she must have. Maybe not the details or the contours, but the idea of who this future person could be, what this place could mean. I can't wait for that woman, the Brooklyn woman I've forgotten, to meet the new Amy, the Detroit Amy I'm still getting to know, and let them merge together, the best of both places.

Home.

I start hanging up the dresses in my closet. Cal and Christian built me a boudoir that I couldn't have even imagined in my dreams. I fully expected this room to be another one of our "someday" projects and that I'd live with a rolling clothes rack and some sheets over the windows for years to come. But Cal, as always, had an idea . . .

"I think we can do this, Amy," he said just a few weeks ago. "I think we can make this work, and you'll have a space where you can sit and drink your coffee and enjoy the morning sun while you read a book. Have you ever read . . . "

And on he trails to talk about the volume of letters between C. S. Lewis, J. R. R. Tolkien, and other writers.

He and Christian ask me a few questions about what I want, but they mostly design the space themselves, evidence in one hundred square feet of how well they've gotten to know me. One wall is lined with floating shelves for shoes, each shelf sitting on a custom-made cleat that mimics the detail of the trim surrounding the windows.

They built the closet by customizing pieces from IKEA, giving me rods for my dresses, blouses, and pants and skirts. There are drawers for my delicates and high shelves for all of my purses, scarves, and hats. Two felt-lined drawers house all of my jewelry. A dedicated light switch illuminates not only the closet but inside the jewelry drawers as well.

I look outside and see Karl out in the backyard, metal pail in hand. He's wearing his orange Tigers cap, cargo shorts, and muck boots. It is warm and muggy after the rain, and he is not wearing a shirt, revealing his thick fur. He looks like such a suburban dad. Never would I have imagined when I was younger that a sight like this would overwhelm me with love. But it does. Still, I wonder what the neighbors must think.

Maddie is laying in a sunbeam as the newest member of our family, Jack the Cat, stalks her in the grass. They will follow Karl around the yard all afternoon as he engages in a quixotic battle with the dandelions. One by one he digs the hardy weeds out of the ground and drops them in his pail. Despite his efforts, there never seem to be fewer of them. The lawn looks like a blanket of white puffs, no matter how diligent he was the day before. "It looks like an invading army," I say to him as I walk out to bring him an iced tea. "We may soon be making sacrifices to their gods."

Or to Jack.

Jack is the neighborhood stray cat that has been coming around almost since we bought the house. In fact, I am almost certain this is the same cat that walked across our roof on that fateful spring day that brought us here. But this winter he really made his presence known. Late on a bitter cold night I could hear caterwauling outside.

"Do you hear that, Karl?" I asked.

"Yeah. Is one of our cats outside?"

"No. I just saw Symba and Dakota in the bedroom."

I peeked out the window and saw Jack sitting on the stoop below, calling to us.

We opened the door, and Jack slunk inside, wild eyed and uncertain but decidedly ready to stay.

Karl prepared a litter box for him in a foil turkey roasting pan, and I found an old cat bed and blanket for him. We didn't know whether he was house-trained, so we shut him into our front vestibule with his bed, box, and bowl. In the morning he shot out the door like a bullet train. But that night he was back, calling to come in. Within weeks he had moved into our bedroom and started coming and going from the house as he pleased. He will disappear for several days at a time and then reappear, as if nothing happened.

He owns us. I'm positive our house will go from Nona's Place to Jack's Place, completely bypassing us in naming rights.

On nice afternoons you can find him lounging on our front stoop, his giant white belly soaking in the heat. If he's caught outside in the rain, he hides in our neighbor's flower urn. When he hears our truck engine idle up, he dashes to our porch and demands to be let in. If we try to walk through the door, he demands to be petted and loved first. If I don't pay the tax, he'll swipe at my ankles. Maddie always gives him wide berth, unsure of the new interloper.

It was Karl who named him Jack.

"As in Jack White?" asked Mary. "You know he lived just a few blocks from here."

Karl shrugged.

"He just seems like a Jack."

But he's not a Jack.

"Hey, that's Amy," a man walking down the street called out to me one morning as I sat on the stoop petting Jack, tufts of his thick white fur floating on the spring breeze.

"What? I'm Amy."

The man pointed to Jack, who is sitting on the stoop with me as I drink my coffee and contemplate what to do about our landscaping. I'm pretty sure the answer is going to be "nothing" again this year, but I can at least say I thought about it.

"That's Amy. He belongs to Timalyn. The woman across the street."

Jack/Amy looked at me.

Fuck.

I think I've stolen the neighbor's cat. I can't help but smile, though, and think of Bear. Technically I also stole Bear, my first dog, from the neighbors. They fed him cat food and left him outside; I "liberated" him with treats. And when they moved away, they left Bear behind for me.

So I've been contemplating what to do about Jack for several weeks, unsure of how to approach Timalyn, whom I don't know well, and confess my transgression. But it's becoming more and more awkward as the weather has gotten warmer and we're all outside more, where she can see Jack lounging on Matilda's stoop.

When I see her outside working in her yard, I decide that today is the day to deal with this. I gather up my courage and walk over.

"I'm Amy," I say, introducing myself.

We've waved on the street but have never been formally intro-duced.

"I'm Timalyn. I think you stole my cat."

"I didn't mean to, I swear! I'm so sorry."

And then I explain how Jack/Amy came to be at our house.

"It's okay," Timalyn says. "He's a roamer. He goes where he likes. And he doesn't like my kids and grandbabies much—it's too much chaos. How about we coparent Amy?"

Coparent a cat? I love it! I thank her profusely for understanding. We're quite attached to Jack. He is our good omen, our sign, after all.

But I can't quite call him Amy. He is definitely a boy cat, and it's too weird having us share a name. So for now he carries two names.

I go around back to tell Karl what happened and find that he's moved on from hunting dandelions to mowing the lawn. Each weekend Karl spends about four hours behind a lawnmower. Proud of his ecosensitivity, he invested in a fancy cordless electric lawnmower. We should have bought the riding variety: not only are we responsible for our lawn, but we also cut the West Village Association's community lot next to us. We are so definitely learning what it means to be homeowners. Being home renovators was just the dating and wooing part; being homeowners is the marriage. Why, I wonder, did mowing the lawn or mopping three thousand square feet never come up in our fantasies?

Up and down the street everyone is losing the battle with dandelions, and the buzz of mowers and edgers recalls the sound of summer across America. What's different here is the bus that just parked up the block and opened its doors, disgorging a dozen volunteers from Detroit's suburbs, come to help the city's less fortunate residents clean up their neighborhoods.

Karl and I look at each other as they come toward us. We're the less fortunate?

It's so absurd, it's funny.

There are plenty of areas across the city that could use some extra hands. But this block isn't one of them.

The volunteers start pulling out rakes and trash bags so they can remove the dead leaves from the small flower garden that commemorates the founders of the West Village Association. Well, if they want to do it instead of us, we'll take the help.

Karl shrugs and goes back to mowing. Maddie trots after him, while Jack reaches out and swats at her tail. She is surprised every time it happens.

◆ ◆ ◆

How different the West Village is in just two years. The people are the same, the energy is the same, but there are new businesses opening and thriving, just like we'd always hoped. Craft Work, owned by our friend Hugh, is a regular stop for fish tacos and old fashioneds during happy hour—our new Fort Defiance. You never know whom you will run into here, as the bar has built a reputation as a welcoming place for the city's power brokers and everyday folk to share cocktails elbow to elbow. The Red Hook, the café our friend from Red Hook had been trying to open since Karl and I first visited friends in the West Village, is finally open. I'm guaranteed to run into a half-dozen people I know each morning as I stand there chatting about life, the universe, and everything with the owner Sandi, her husband, Andy, and my favorite baristas. There is Detroit Vegan Soul, whose co-owners, Erika and Kirsten, have catered some of our parties and serve the most delicious southern-fried tofu bites. The restaurant is always hopping on evenings when it does spoken-word poetry jams, and it's nice to see so much vibrancy. Tarot & Tea is a calm oasis on the block. I pop my head in on occasion, always finding center in Nefertiti's shop. A few blocks away is the Parker Street Market, where I find the Dave's Sweet Tooth almond toffee I'm addicted to. David carries all of the basics in his organic bodega as well as a curated selection of Detroit-made brands, giving many small producers their first shot at retail. And now, across the street, there's Sister Pie, opened by another new friend, Lisa.

On the night of Sister Pie's grand opening, Karl and I drive over, having just finished a long walk on Belle Isle. The spring evening is crisp and stormy, more like October than May. It starts to pour just as we pull up, and we race to the storefront that until just recently had brown butcher's paper hanging in the windows. The inside renovations are finally revealed. We can see people standing everywhere, something that hasn't happened in this space in a very long time. We know almost everyone inside and are greeted with hugs and enthusiasm. It feels good to feel like we belong, to be a part of this celebratory event in our neighborhood, and to look out the window and see the city that is our home.

When the rain lets up and the sun reappears, the party spills out the front door, everyone with glasses of champagne or Lisa's famous buckwheat chocolate chip cookies in hand. We look down Kercheval Street to the east and see a giant double rainbow that appears to dead end right at the block. I've never been so close to the end of the rainbow, and it is brilliant, like we can almost touch the pot of gold. It seems like a good omen for Lisa and her new business and for our neighborhood and the next phase of its life. The chatter at the party is that a new French bistro will be opening as well as another restaurant and more retail. All of these new establishments will be sprouting in buildings that had been more derelict than Matilda when we first saw her. Everything is changing.

But standing in this party, filled with beautiful people I love, all of whom have the best of hearts and intentions for their lives and this city, I can't help but notice that we are a gaggle of all-white faces.

People keep saying how great it is for the neighborhood to develop into what they envisioned and dreamed it would be. Some people in the conversations are neighbors who have been here for years; others have arrived more recently than Karl and me.

I don't know what I had hoped for this neighborhood. I wanted change to come, certainly. I wanted to see the vacant buildings teeming with life again. I want our friends' children to be able to ride their bikes up to Sister Pie or Red Hook for a treat. I like that our neighborhood is rebuilding its retail core, the small business owners becoming the fabric of our lives. But I didn't expect so much development quite so quickly. It feels a little unsettling. I thought we'd have time to work together and to ensure as a community that the spaces were filled by a diverse group of business owners. I am thrilled for everyone who has opened. I count them among my friends and patronize their businesses frequently. But I want to make sure that the old-time businesses, like the black barber Karl goes to, Heavy Weight Cuts, isn't forgotten about. Few men in the neighborhood patronize Dave; most don't even know he exists. When they hear Karl goes there, they are all curious, interested, but not sure they could go in. But Karl made it a point to start going as soon as we moved into Matilda. It's nothing fancy, but it's Dave's shop, a place he loves, and we want to ensure it has a place in this community. We don't want it pushed out in favor of a luxury handbag store or one of the fancy barbershops with forty-dollar cuts that have opened recently in downtown and Midtown. I want his voice to be heard, for him to be as important a part of the conversation about the future as some of us here at the Sister Pie grand opening. I don't want him to be a casualty of the future.

I want that rainbow, that omen, to be for all of Detroit. I feel like things are improving, but I know they may only be improving for people who look like me or who have means like me. I don't know what the answers are, but I'm insisting on having the hard, sometimes uncomfortable conversations. How as a city do we take the lessons of Brooklyn, San Francisco, Seattle, Denver—all those booming "winner" cities—and apply what works and jettison the things that bring inequality? How do we make sure we do not continue to be one of the centers of America's forgotten people and places? The questions I started asking in Ann Arbor just three years ago still ring true and urgent now.

As more newcomers arrive in the city, I am having weekly coffee dates with people seeking my advice on navigating the complexities of Detroit. It was a novelty when I met with Amy, and now it's a regularity. Some of them want to hear real talk, and others just want pure boosterism. I find myself walking a fine line between encouragement and reality. I want to give people the tools to succeed and also the knowledge not to fail. How do I be a modern-day Jim Boyle for the new people who are arriving just as naive as Karl and I were? Sometimes I find myself succeeding, and other times I fail spectacularly.

Because it's such a complicated city, I'm not always sure where to start. I try to be real, to give them an honest assessment of the opportunities and challenges. I think about the Boyles and how they simultaneously encouraged us and were forthcoming. How much did they reveal, and how much did they hold back for us to discover on our own? It's hard to strike the right tone, as I am still seeking answers. I will likely always be seeking and learning to live with the fact that I am both gentrified and gentrifier. That it will be a lifelong meditation is not necessarily something new arrivals want to hear. I end up scaring some as I try to have a nuanced discussion about how issues of race and class layer together with a sense of distrust, making it difficult at times to navigate the rocky shoals of becoming an "us" in a way that is deft and respectful. I try to explain that it is important to take Detroit for what it is, not try to mold it to suit. But that doesn't mean not doing anything. New businesses, new ideas, new energy are all welcome. Just don't be disrespectful in the pursuit.

I want to save them the mistakes so many have made before, show them the landmines Karl and I have triggered so they can avoid them and evolve more quickly. I try to explain the idea of cultural gentrification and how using the words *help* and *save* may be offensive here. I want to warn them about the hate and anger that overwhelmed me for a period before I learned to better navigate and to listen. But that often doesn't go over well. I'm trying to have calculus-level conversations with people ready for fractions.

How can save *be offensive*? they ask.

Because, Detroit, I want to reply.

One woman arrives and tells me she is starting her own business and expects people to put aside any of their past issues so we can all work together to move forward. I try to explain that although the sentiment sounds good on paper, it is a bit arrogant to come into a new city and declare what people should do just because you arrived. It's always easier when you're the one leading the conversation and can pretend all that happened before never did. Nobody wants to get stuck in the past, let it stymie us, but by not acknowledging the city's realities, what people went through in modern history, we can never truly understand each other.

Let's just say this woman and I never came to an understanding.

"If you hate Detroit so much, why are you here?" she asked. "Why don't you just leave? Why are you so negative?"

"I love Detroit," I replied, feeling slapped. "This is my home. But it's complicated. I'm just trying to explain."

We hugged good-bye after an awkward lunch, both uncertain with the other.

She didn't want to hear, nobody wants hear, the alternative to the popular narrative that the city is rebounding. When people are still new and excited, they don't want to hear that they likely won't get a loan to fix up the cheap house they just bought. They think I'm making it up or am just being negative. But I'm not. This is a very real battle we must solve. Ownership is key to this city's future. Who can—and cannot—buy now may rechart Detroit's course. It is imperative that we get housing policy right this time and not repeat the mistakes of our exclusionary past. We must all focus on the work of justice and inequality as much as entrepreneurship and new opportunities. These are not easy problems to solve, but if they were, Detroiters would have solved them long ago. This is a place just oozing with passionate, committed, and talented people.

Karl and I aren't here to change or save Detroit. We love it for what it is, not what it might be. We want city services, yes. But we want them for everyone. We want to be here and demand better for this city and all its residents because we all deserve that. Karl and I want a thriving Detroit with businesses opening and investment happening. We want there to be jobs for everyone, not just newcomers like us with college degrees. After all, we're betting on the Motor City; we've tied our futures to its future. We don't want those who have never left to be pushed out of the way by us and our dreams. We are choosing to live in a place where privilege can be defined as having a job, and I believe that our choice comes with deep responsibilities.

"Experience can make you jaded or cynical, and then it's time to go," Cal once told me. "But you have the other side, where you are fresh but have no experience or depth of understanding of what it's taken to get here. You need experience plus compassion. That is wisdom. The two camps rarely ever walk a mile in each other's shoes to really understand what it's like."

◆ ◆ ◆

I shut our front door, pleased each time with the satisfying thud it makes against the copper weather stripping Cal installed. The door is a testament to everything that has happened over the past two years. We took something decrepit and unloved and filled it with life thanks to the help of our partners and friends. Gary rebuilt the original door. Christian painstakingly painted it a rich black-green. And Cal installed a new brass spyglass that is an exact replica of the original. I'm sometimes moved to tears by how handsome our front door is. There is still work to be done on Matilda—we're still missing the corbel right above the entrance and we need gutters—but the door to our house, to our home and hearts, stands strong and inviting.

I hurry to catch up with Karl, who is walking down the middle of Van Dyke Place, heading to our friends' porch. Nick and Ellen live around the corner, and most weekends, now that the weather is warm, there is a migration up and down the block between neighbors' porches and stoops. Sometimes we stop for a beer next door at Tommy and Elle's. The Boyle family will see us and come over. George and Sheila stop by to chat. Then maybe Kevin and Liz Towner will wander by on a walk with their baby and get distracted from their original mission. Then the Dorns come by with their kids in tow. Mark and Kathy Beltaire and Carol and Bob Rhodes, our patron saints of the block, are always game for a strolling, roving evening of community. Sometimes you're just trying to take a walk, and you get sucked in for a good, long porch-sit. I think of Red Hook, when it took us an hour to make a ten-minute walk.

Karl has a six-pack of homebrew with him, and I follow with mason jars of gin and tonics. Maddie is up ahead, allowed to walk off-leash to Nick's house. They love her there. Nick sends us home if we don't bring Maddie, even to more formal events we've shared with them, like Christmas Eve. Maddie dog is the beloved, just as she was in Red Hook.

But she has competition for the affection. Jaunting along next to Maddie is Jack cat, the neighborhood superstar. He likes to come to the parties too. When we arrive at Nick and Ellen's, Jack stakes out a step and then lolls about on it all evening, only moving when he wants to find a higher perch. When we leave, I call Maddie to come, and Jack falls in line, the Haimerl-Kaebnick family making their way home.

It is amazing how life works out sometimes. Karl and I ended up here in the West Village by chance—it wasn't even on our short list of neighborhoods—and yet we've landed in exactly the perfect place. It's not a new Red Hook, but it's our Detroit. It is more than just a place where people live. It is a community.

People help one another here. Residents care for their properties, sweeping porches and planting flowers, even when the abandoned property next door is fire ravaged and teetering dangerously close to collapsing on their own roof. They mow the vacant lots the city has forsaken. They plant community gardens and invite neighbors to eat from the harvest.

Here in the West Village, neighbors wave and greet each other. We call to each other across neat lawns and past freshly painted fences, across the scorched remains of abandoned houses and past alleyways filled with trash, tires, mattresses, and even boats. Over porches bursting with pots of flowering geraniums and past driveways lined with flaming-orange daylilies. *Good evening,* we say, whether we face beauty or decay. *Good morning,* we call. Ever watchful of who and what is walking down our block.

Just like Marsha Music said: "Just say hi."

And we do.

ACKNOWLEDGMENTS

I am but one woman surrounded by hundreds who have helped to make *Detroit Hustle* a reality. This book is as much a testament to them as it is the labor of my love. First and foremost, I must thank my parents, Dick and Laurelle Haimerl. Without them I am nothing. Thank you for everything, even the hard stuff, Mom and Dad.

To my husband, Karl, I am forever grateful. A woman couldn't have a better partner in life. You were kind and patient and offered unwavering support throughout this project. You believed in me even when I couldn't believe in myself. Thank you for being my Lovey.

To Cal and Christian Garfield, I cannot thank you enough for the care and passion you put into Matilda. We couldn't have found better partners to make this dream—and so much more—a reality.

To my superb agent, Melissa Sarver White, thank you times one million for your enthusiasm and support for this project. You are my gladiator. Thank you for bringing this book to the wonderful team at Running Press. I am indebted to Sophia Muthuraj for acquiring *Detroit Hustle* and pushing me to tell a memoir, not just a nonfiction narrative, about making a life in Detroit. And finally, to my editor, Lisa Kaufman: a girl couldn't have a better partner in publishing than you. My book is infinitely better thanks to your probing questions and witty insights. Please enjoy a PBR tonight.

To Stacy Cowley, thank you for always having my back and always tolerating my adventures even as you want to murder me. You're an honorary Detroiter now.

Of course, there would be no book without the city of Detroit and the people who call her home. To them I offer my deepest thanks. Although not everyone I've met appears in these pages, every person lives in my heart. Your stories helped shape mine, and I am forever in your debt. There are a few people whose guidance was instrumental, and I would like to publicly thank them: to Leslie

Lynn Smith for being a mentor and a friend whose commitment to equity and inclusion inspires me daily; to Dave Egner for giving me courage when mine was waning; to Joanne Gerstner for keeping me in wine, *Scandal*, and good friendship when it was desperately needed; to Carla Walker Miller for her straight talk about what has been, what is, and what could come; to Beth Niblock for our shared love of cowboy boots and struggle through newcomer status; to Vittoria Katanski for her amazing laugh and gimlet eye; to Mary Lorene Carter and Pasta Batman for too many nights, too, too late, at PJs and all that comes with it; to Mark and Kathy Beltaire, Bob and Carol Rhodes, Jim Boyle and Mary Trybus, Tommy Simon and Elle Gotham, Josh and Jessica Dorn, George and Sheila Robinson, Liz and Kevin Towner, Cynthia Jankowski, and Charlie Nordstrom and Dara O'Byrne for being the best neighbors two Brooklyn transplants could hope for; to Nick Assenmacher and Ellen Barrett for their perfect porch, sense of adventure, and skill with a pig roast; to Lisa Michelle Waud and Jason Vogel, our first friends in Michigan, for making us feel welcome and want to stay; to Alexis Wiley for being a friend even when we were on opposite sides; to Martina Guzman for keeping me in tamales and good conversation when it was most needed; to Devita Davison and April Boyle for bringing the fight and demanding better every day; to Craig Fahle for teaching me the ropes on radio and always taking my call; to Katy Locker for excellent writing distractions such as Nick Cave and so much more; to Marsha Music for blessing this city with her writing and allowing me to use a small piece of it in this book; to Charles Eisendrath, Birgit Rieck, and the entire Knight Wallace family for embarking with us on this adventure; and finally, to Mary Kramer, Cindy Goodaker, Jeannette Smith, and the entire team at *Crain's Detroit Business*, I couldn't have done this book without your patience and support.

Before Detroit, however, so many people touched my life and mentored me at critical points so that I could go from a girl in a trailer to a published author. I'd like to thank those editors and teachers who have been instrumental: Donna Ladd, Todd Stauffer, Patty Calhoun, Lowell "Papa" Sharp, Ron Finelli, Zav and Khushnur Dadabhoy, Dr. Oneida Meranto, Dr. Robert Hazan, Dr. John Cochran, Dr. Arthur A. Fleisher III, Mrs. Hull, Mrs. Martenuska, and Mrs. Furphy.

Thank you all.